Satoto Endar Nayono

Anaerobic digestion of organic solid waste for energy production

AF286767

Karlsruher Berichte zur Ingenieurbiologie
Band 46

Institut für Ingenieurbiologie und Biotechnologie
des Abwassers
Karlsruher Institut für Technologie

Herausgeber: Prof. Dr. rer. nat. J. Winter

Anaerobic digestion of organic solid waste for energy production

by
Satoto Endar Nayono

Dissertation, genehmigt von der
Fakultät für Bauingenieur-, Geo- und Umweltwissenschaften
der Universität Fridericiana zu Karlsruhe (TH)
Tag der mündlichen Prüfung: 11. Dezember 2009
Referenten: Prof. Dr. rer. nat. Josef Winter, Prof. Dr.–Ing. E.h. Herman H. Hahn

Impressum

Karlsruher Institut für Technologie (KIT)
KIT Scientific Publishing
Straße am Forum 2
D-76131 Karlsruhe
www.uvka.de

KIT – Universität des Landes Baden-Württemberg und nationales
Forschungszentrum in der Helmholtz-Gemeinschaft

KIT Scientific Publishing 2010
Print on Demand

ISSN: 0172-8709
ISBN: 978-3-86644-464-5

Foreword

The work presented in this doctoral dissertation was conducted at the *Institut für Inginieurbiologie und Biotechnology des Abwassers* at Universität Karlsruhe (TH) from October 2005 to September 2009. This PhD study was financially supported by scholarship grants from the International Postgraduate Studies in Water Technologies (IPSWaT) organized by the International Bureau of the BMBF (*Bundesministerium für Bildung und Forschung*). The final year support was obtained from *Landesstiftung Baden-Württemberg*.

This dissertation presents the most important results of my doctoral work, which partly have been published or prepared as journal manuscripts. These manuscripts are:

1. Nayono, S.E., Gallert, C. and Winter, J., 2009. Foodwaste as a Co-Substrate in a Fed-Batch Anaerobic Biowaste Digester for Constant Biogas Supply. *Water Science and Technology*. Vol. 59 (6): 1169–1178, doi:10.2166/wst.2009.102

2. Nayono, S.E., Winter, J. and Gallert, C., 2009. Anaerobic Digestion of Pressed Off Leachate from the Organic Fraction of Municipal Solid Waste. *Waste Management*, doi:10.1016/j.wasman.2009.09.019

3. Nayono, S.E., Gallert, C. and Winter, J., 2009. Anaerobic Co-Digestion of Biowaste with Press Water and Foodwaste for the Improvement of Biogas Production. (in preparation, to be submitted to *Bioresource Technology*)

In addition to those manuscripts, the results from the experiment of the potential use of potato sludge as a substrate in anaerobic digester are also included. Other results of this work such as piles of fatty acids GC papers, MS-Excel data files, new knowledge from hundreds of journal articles as well as headache caused by the technical problems of the reactors and laboratory equipments (not to mention the explosions of assays and biowaste) are not presented here. However, everybody who does such laboratory work will understand that all of the results will only fit in thousands of pages.

In general, the process of this doctoral study provided me a lot of knowledge and valuable experiences not only for my scientific life in the future but also my daily life. I do realize that this dissertation cannot be completed without a full support from the people around me. Therefore, it is a pleasure to thank those who made this dissertation possible.

First of all, I would like to express my special gratitude to my supervisor, Prof. Dr. rer.nat. Josef Winter, for his supervision, advice, and guidance from the very early stage of this study as well as giving me this very interesting topic of research. He also provided me encouragement and even non-technical supports whenever necessary. I am indebted to him more than he knows. I gratefully acknowledge Prof. Dr.-Ing. E.h. Hermann H. Hahn, Ph.D. for agreeing to be the *Korreferent* of my dissertation. His lecture on sanitation technology during my master course in Resources Engineering inspired me to be further involved in the field of sanitation engineering. My special thanks go to Prof. Dr. sc. agr. Dieter Prinz for willing to be a member in the examination committee. Back to 2002, Professor Prinz gave me the possibility to enjoy the nice course in Resources Engineering and provided me a lot of support in various ways. I owe my sincere gratitude to PD Dr. rer. nat Claudia Gallert for her valuable hints and constructive comments on my work. From her I learned a lot of things related to laboratory work.

I would like to acknowledge Dr. Ulrike Schaub (former IPSWaT coordinator) and Hr. Achim Niessen (*Akademisches Auslandamt*, Uni-Karlsruhe) for honoring me with the scholarships. The financial support offered me a precious opportunity to broaden my knowledge and helped me to pursue my dreams in the future.

I was fortune to have worked with colleagues who were very supportive and created a pleasant working atmosphere. I am very thankful to Fr. Renate Anschütz who helped me in doing some laboratory analysis; to Fr. Rita Seith for helping me in administration matters and Daniel Jost for helping me improving the german abstract. My best thanks also go to all former and present colleagues at the *Institut für Inginieurbiologie und Biotechnology des Abwassers* for their scientific support and friendship.

This work would not have been possible without the support and continuous prayer from my mother, parents in law, brothers and sisters. Last but not least, I would like to thank my beloved family. Innumerable encouragement and moral support from my wife Tanti Nayono and our joyful daughter Carla and son Hadrian are powerful sources of inspiration and energy. To them, this work is dedicated.

Satoto E. Nayono   Karlsruhe, 2009

Abstract

The total amount of municipal solid waste is continuously rising. Consequently, there are millions of tons of solid waste being produced every year which have to be safely disposed without any negative impact to the environment. On the other hand, as one of the driving forces for economic and social development the availability of energy in sufficient and sustainable amount has been becoming world's main interest. However, depending on the way the energy is produced, distributed and used, it may contribute to environmental problems such as water, land and air pollution or even global climate change. Anaerobic digestion as a pre-treatment prior to landfill disposal or composting offers several advantages, such as minimization of masses and volume, inactivation of biological and biochemical processes in order to avoid landfill-gas and odor emissions, reduction of landfill settlements and energy production in the form of methane. Therefore, anaerobic digestion of bio-degradable solid wastes can be considered an alternative option to improve the environment condition caused by organic solid waste and at the same time taking an advantage as an environmentally-friendly resource of energy.

This study was carried out in order to evaluate the performance of anaerobic reactors treating OFMSW (organic fraction of municipal solid waste), especially in terms of its energy recovery, either by investigating the maximum organic loading rate or by co-digestion with other types of wastes for energy recovery. In order to reach the research purpose, several experimental activities such as characteristics examination of different organic solid wastes, which are potential substrates for anaerobic digestion and performance evaluation of the anaerobic reactors treating OFMSW were initiated. The Except for source-sorted OFMSW (later called biowaste), the substrates examined in this study were pressing leachate from an OFMSW composting plant (press water), source-sorted foodwaste (foodwaste), and excess sludge from a potato industry wastewater treatment plant (potato sludge).

The substrates examined were found to be readily degradable with relatively high methane production potentials. Foodwaste could be considered as a suitable supplementary substrate for a semi continuously-fed biowaste digester during night times and as the sole substrate during weekends when no biowaste is processed in order to equilibrate biogas production. The total biogas production of the reactor increased by 21-37 % when the substrates were fed in addition to biowaste compared to biogas production during biowaste-only-feed periods during the day and no feeding during the night. The COD elimination efficiency of the reactor reached the same level as in biowaste-only-feed periods (51–65 %). The volatile solids elimination efficiency was between 62 – 65 %, which was insignificantly less compared to the volatile solids elimination during biowaste-only-feed periods (63 – 68 %).

As a sole substrate, press water could be fed to an anaerobic digester up to a maximum OLR of 27.7 kg COD $\cdot m^{-3} \cdot d^{-1}$. During the digestion, a stable elimination of organic material (measured as COD elimination) of approximately 60 % was achieved with a maximum biogas production of 7.1 $m^3 \cdot m^{-3}_{reactor} \cdot d^{-1}$. Considering the optimum VS elimination, the COD removal efficiency, the problem caused by formation of massive foam at higher OLR and a reserve capacity for an increased amount of press water in the future, it is suggested that anaerobic digestion of press water should be operated at an OLR within the range of 13.5 to 22.5 kg COD $\cdot m^{-3} \cdot d^{-1}$. A net surplus energy of about 10.8 kWh may be obtained from each ton OFMSW delivered when an anaerobic digester for press water is operated at an OLR of 21.3 kg COD $\cdot m^{-3} \cdot d^{-1}$ (HRT: 10 days).

The results of anaerobic co-digestion of biowaste with press water or foodwaste showed that the addition of these co-substrates not only linearly increased biogas production but also improved the biogas production rates. An increase of the OLR by 10.9 % during co-digestion with press water for instance, increased the biogas production as much as 18.3 % (the biogas production rate improved by 7.3 % compared to the OLR by biowaste suspension only). The addition of press water or foodwaste as a co-substrate also resulted in significant increase of the digestate's buffer capacity, which enables the operation of anaerobic digestion without an additional pH control system. Considering several factors, the optimum addition of press water and foodwaste is suggested at 15–20 % and 10–15 % by volume, respectively.

Potato sludge has a relatively high organic matter content. The volatile solids content of the sludge reached about 22 % of the total weight. It had a maximum methane production of around 0.40 m^3 $CH_4 \cdot kg^{-1}$ VS. More than 80 % of its maximum methane production in batch assays was achieved within the first 4 days of incubation indicating that it was easily degradable. The concentrations of heavy metals in the potato sludge were lower than the inhibitory or toxic concentration limit. More than 70 % of its volatile solids were eliminated during solid elimination tests. Therefore, potato sludge is considered as suitable for anaerobic digestion either as a sole substrate or co-substrate.

Zusammenfassung

Das Gesamtvolumen von kommunalen und industriellen Abfällen ist kontinuierlich steigend. Millioner Tonnen Abfälle werden jährlich produziert, die ohne negative Auswirkungen auf die Umwelt entsorgt werden müssen. Auf der anderen Seite ist die Verfügbarkeit von Energie in ausreichender und nachhaltiger Menge ein globales Interesse. Allerdings, je nachdem wie die Energie produziert, verteilt und verwendet wird, kann es zu Umweltproblemen wie Wasser-, Boden- und Luftverschmutzung oder sogar zu globalem Klimawandel führen. Eine anaerobe Vergärung von Biomüll als Vorbehandlung vor der Deponierung oder Kompostierung der organischen Fraktion bietet mehrere Vorteile, z.B. die Minimierung von Massen und Volumen, die Vermeidung von Deponiegas- und Geruchsemissionen, die Reduzierung von Reaktionen nach Stabilisierung und die Methangewinnung für Energieproduktion. Daher kann die anaerobe Vergärung von biologisch abbaubaren Abfällen zur Verbesserung der Umwelt beitragen und gleichzeitig das entstehende Methan als umweltfreundliche Energieressource dienen.

Diese Studie wurde durchgeführt, um die Leistung der anaeroben Vergärung von OFMSW (Engl.: _o_rganic _f_raction of _m_unicipal _s_olid _w_aste: organische Fraktion der Kommunalabfälle) zu charakterisieren. Die Studie konzentriert sich auf die Biogasproduktion von Abfällen, entweder durch die Untersuchung der maximal möglichen organischen Belastung oder durch die Co-Vergärung mit anderen Arten von Abfällen. Die Substrate in dieser Studie waren: Getrennt gesammelter Bioabfall (später _Biowaste_ genannt), Sickerwasser aus der _OFMSW_ einer Kompostierungsanlage (_Press water_), getrennt gesammelte Speisereste (_Foodwaste_) und Überschuss-schlamm aus einer Kläranlage der Kartoffelindustrie (_Potato sludge_).

Die Substrate erwiesen sich als leicht abbaubar und haben ein relativ hohes Methanproduktionspotenzial. Foodwaste könnte als ein zusätzliches Substrat für eine semi-kontinuierlich gefütterte Biogasanlage in der Nacht und als alleiniges Substrat an den Wochenenden dienen, um die Erzeugung von Biogas relativ konstant zu halten. Durch Zugabe von _Foodwaste_ in der Nacht, erhöht sich die Biogasproduktion des Reaktors um 21-37 %. Die CSB-Abbauleistung des Reaktors blieb auf dem gleichen Niveau wie ohne Co-Vergärung (51-65 %). Die oTS-Elimination während der Co-Vergärungszeit lag zwischen 62 bis 65 % und war somit nur geringfügig kleiner als der Wert der oTS-Elimination bei der Monovergärung von _OFMSW_ (63 – 68 %).

Als einziges Substrat für einen anaeroben Bioreaktor konnte *Press water* bis zu einer maximalen OLR von 27,7 kg COD $\cdot m^{-3} \cdot d^{-1}$ gefüttert werden. Während der Vergärung wurde eine stabile Elimination von organischem Material von ca. 60 % (als CSB gemessen) mit einer maximalen Biogasproduktion von 7,1 $m^3 \cdot m^{-3} \cdot d^{-1}$ erreicht. In Anbetracht der optimalen VS-Elimination, der CSB-Abbau Effizienz, der Probleme durch die Bildung von massivem Schaum bei höheren OLRs und der Notwendigkeit einer Reservekapazität für eine erhöhte zukünftige Menge von *Press water*, wird vorgeschlagen, die anaerobe Vergärung von *Press water* auf eine OLR im Bereich von 13,5 bis 22,5 kg CSB $\cdot m^{-3} \cdot d^{-1}$ festzulegen. Eine Überschuss Energie von etwa 10,8 kWh kann aus jeder Tonne *OFMSW* erzielt werden, wenn ein anaerober Bioreaktor mit dem *Press water* bei einer OLR von 21,3 kg COD $\cdot m^{-3} \cdot d^{-1}$ betrieben wird.

Die Ergebnisse der anaeroben Co-Vergärung zeigten, dass durch die Beigabe der Co-Substrate die Biogasproduktionsrate überproportional verbesserte wurde. Ein Zusatz von 10,9 % OLR, während der Co-Vergärung mit z.B. *Press water*, erhöhte die Erzeugung von Biogas um 18,3 % (die Biogasproduktionsrate verbesserte sich um 7,3 % gegenüber der OLR von *Biowaste* als alleinigem Substrat). Die Zugabe von *Press water* oder *Foodwaste* als Co-Substrat führte auch zu einer signifikanten Zunahme der Puffer-Kapazität des Gärgutes, die den Betrieb der anaeroben Vergärung ohne zusätzliches pH-Kontrolle-System ermöglicht. Unter Berücksichtigung verschiedener Faktoren, wird optimalerweise die Zugabe von 15-20 % *Press water* und 10-15 % *Foodwaste* vorgeschlagen.

Potato sludge hatte einen relativ hohen Gehalt an organischer Substanz. Die organische Trockensubstanz des Schlamms betrug etwa 22 % des Gesamtgewichts. Die maximale Methanproduktion betrug 0,40 m^3 $CH_4 \cdot kg^{-1}$ oTS. Mehr als 80 % der maximalen Methanmenge wurde in den ersten 4 Tagen produziert. Die Konzentrationen von Schwermetallen im *Potato sludge* waren niedriger als die hemmende oder toxische Konzentration. Mehr als 70 % der oTS wurde während des oTS-Eliminations-Tests eliminiert. Daher ist *Potato sludge* geeignet für die anaerobe Vergärung entweder als alleiniges Substrat oder als Co-Substrat.

Table of contents

List of tables

List of figures

List of abbreviations

3R	: Reduction, recycling, resources recovery
AD	: Anaerobic digestion
BOD	: Biochemical oxygen demand
C/N ratio	: Carbon-nitrogen ratio
CHP	: Combined heat and power
COD	: Chemichal oxygen demand
CSTR	: Completely stirred tank reactor
EC	: European Commission
EEA	: European Environment Agency
h	: Hour
HRT	: Hydraulic retertion time
kWh	: Kilowatt hour
MBT	: Mechanical and biological treatment
MJ	: Mega Joule
OECD	: Organisation for Economic Co-operation and Development
OFMSW	: Organic fraction of municipal solid waste
OLR	: Organic loading rate
OME	: Oil mill effluent waste
SRB	: Sulfate-reducing bacteria
TKN	: Total Kjehdahl nitrogen
TS	: Total solids
TSS	: Total suspended solids
UNFPA	: United Nations Fund for Population Activities
VFA	: Volatile fatty acids
VS	: Volatile solids

Chapter 1

INTRODUCTION

1.1 The world population and solid waste generation

According to a prognosis from the United Nations (2007), the world population will likely increase by 2.5 billion over the next 40 years, passing from the current 6.7 billion to 9.2 billion in 2050. This population increase is equivalent to the world's population in 1950 and will be absorbed mostly by the less developed countries, whose population is projected to rise from 5.4 billion in 2007 to 7.9 billion in 2050. In contrast, the population of the more developed countries is expected to remain stable at 1.2 billion. In 2008, more than half world's population, 3.3 billion people, lived in urban areas. By 2030, the number is expected to increase to almost 5 billion. Already in the year 2000, there were at least 23 mega cities with population of more than 10 million. Most of these cities were located in developing countries (UNFPA, 2007).

As a consequence to the increasing number of population and the improvement of living quality since the past three decades, the total amount of municipal solid waste is continuously rising. An annual rise of solid waste amount of about 2 - 3 % can be estimated (Salhofer *et al.*, 2007). The OECD (2004) reported that the generation of municipal solid waste within OECD members increased by approximately 54% between 1980 and 2000. In Europe alone, it is estimated that more than 3,000 million tons of waste are generated annually (EEA, 2003). Out of this number, 60 million tons of recyclable organic wastes are collected from households and food industries (Barth *et al.*, 1998 in Gallert and Winter, 2002).

The similar trend of increasing municipal solid waste amounts is also observed in the other part of the world. Consequently, there are millions of tons of solid waste being produced every year which have to be disposed. Especially in the less developed countries, caused by the lack of know-how and financial support, most of the solid wastes are treated and disposed improperly. These practices lead to several problems such as aesthetical problems (odour nuisance, turbid water, *etc.*), health problems (skin infection, diarrhoea, breeding of pathogenic vectors, *etc.*) and environmental problems (damage to surface or ground water due to leachate production, eutrophication, soil contamination, air pollution due to improper incinerator or "smoking-landfills", *etc.*).

1.2 Solid waste management hierarchy

Due to the environmental problems caused by solid waste generation, during the last 30 years solid waste management has become a major concern around the world. The main tool of integrated solid waste management is solid waste management hierarchy. This management hierarchy consists of a comprehensive waste reduction, recycling, resources recovery (commonly known as 3R strategies) and final treatment/disposal (Bagchi, 2004; Cheriminisoff, 2003).

Waste reduction is aimed to prevent waste from being generated. The strategies of waste reduction include using less packaging, designing products to last longer, and reusing products and materials. Recycling of solid waste involves collecting, reprocessing, and/or recovering certain waste materials (*e.g.*, glass, metal, plastics, paper) to make new materials or products. Resources recovery includes recovery of organic materials which are rich in nutrients and can be used to improve soils (composting) and the conversion of certain types of waste into useful energy such as heat and electricity (anaerobic digestion).

When the solid waste cannot be prevented or minimized through 3R strategy, the next strategy is reducing solid waste volume and/or its toxicity before ultimate disposal. One way to reduce the volume of solid waste is through combustion. Combustion facilities can produce steam that can be used to generate energy. The ultimate disposal of solid waste is to place it in landfills. If the technology is available, properly designed, constructed, and managed landfills can be used to generate energy by recovering its methane production.

1.3 Rationale of anaerobic digestion of solid waste

Due to its simplicity and financial reason, solid waste disposal on sanitary landfill has been the common practice for many decades. However, a study of Eriksson *et al.*, (2005) shows that reducing landfilling in favour of increasing recycle of energy and materials lead to a lower environmental impact, a lower consumption of energy resources, and lower economic costs. Landfilling of energy-rich waste should be avoided as far as possible, partly because of the negative environmental impacts from landfilling, and mainly because of its low recovery of resources. Furthermore, burying organic fraction of municipal solid waste together with other fractions implied extra cost for leachate treatment, low biogas quality and quantity, and high post closure care.

In Europe the introduction of the European Landfill Directive (EC, 1999) has stimulated European Union Member States to develop sustainable solid waste management strategies, including collection, pre-treatment and final treatment methods. According to the Directive, it is compulsory for the Member States to reduce the amount of biodegradable solid waste that is deposited on sanitary landfills. Thus by the year 2020 there will be only less than 35 % of the total biodegradable solid wastes that were produced in 1995 being deposited on sanitary landfills.

Separation of municipal waste into a recyclable fraction, residual waste and a source-sorted organic fraction is a common practice option of waste management adopted by the European Union Member States in order to meet the obligations of the Landfill Directive. In Germany, for instance, in 2006 around 8.45 million tons of OFMSW were collected. It consisted of 4.15 million tons of source-sorted organic household residues and 4.3 million tons of compostable solid waste from gardens and parks (Statistisches Bundesamt, 2008a). Due to the high moisture content and low caloric value of organic waste, incineration will not be an economical option. Thus, the treatment of OFMSW can be realized alternatively by anaerobic digestion or aerobic composting. There are 1742 biological treatment plants and 45 mechanical-biological treatment plants throughout Germany, including composting plants and anaerobic digesters (Statistisches Bundesamt, 2008b).

Compared to composting, anaerobic digestion of OFMSW has several advantages, such as better handling of wet waste, the possibility of energy recovery in the form of methane, less area requirement and less emission of bad odor and green house gasses (Baldasano and Soriano, 2000; Hartmann and Ahring, 2006). Furthermore, if the digestate of an anaerobic digester has to be disposed in a landfill, anaerobic digestion of OFMSW has advantages such as: minimization of masses and volume, inactivation of biological and biochemical processes in order to avoid landfill-gas and odor emissions, reduction of landfill settlements, and immobilization of pollutants in order to reduce leachate contamination (Fricke *et al.*, 2005).

1.4   The example of waste-to-energy concept in the city of Karlsruhe

For treatment of source-sorted biowaste from cities such as Karlsruhe/Germany, anaerobic digestion with biogas production for steam and electricity supply has been installed in full-scale (Gallert *et al.*, 2003). To maintain a permanent energy supply for the customers, biogas must be available at constant amounts 24 h a day. This can be reached by supplementary biogas sources, for instance from a sanitary landfill or by steam generation from incineration of waste wood, as realized in Karlsruhe. The combination of biogas from biowaste and biogas from sanitary landfills even works at closed landfills, when the gas production has passed its peak amounts. Whereas gas storage is limited and costly, waste wood incineration is flexible and could serve for steam and electricity supply during shortage of biowaste or revision periods of bioreactors. The treatment of biowaste and the incineration of waste wood at the site of a (closed) sanitary landfill has the advantage, that traffic infrastructure exists already and occasional odour problems can be minimized, since the distance towards neighbouring settlements is far enough. The use of landfill gas and biogas from the biowaste digestion plant as well as the use of heat from wood waste incineration for electricity and steam supply (see Figure 1.1) is expected to contribute to the reduction of carbon dioxide emission and reduce dependency on fossil fuel.

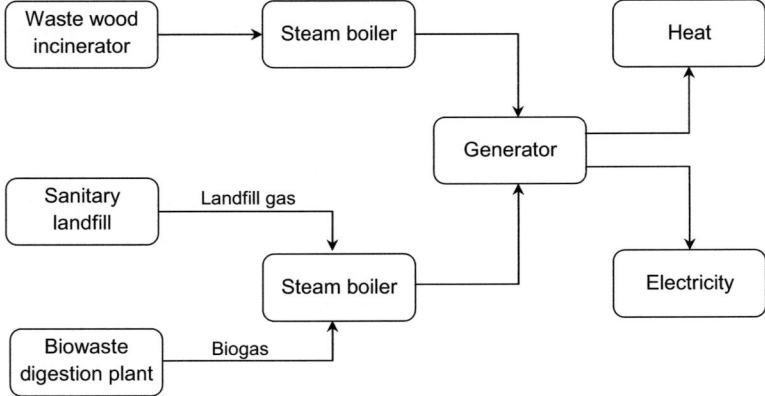

Figure 1.1 Schematic diagram of a "waste to energy" concept which is applied in the city of Karlsruhe

Since landfill gas reaches its peak production approximately 10 years after closure and later on the amount of landfill gas (and its quality) will decrease significantly (Lee and Jones-Lee, 1999). Generator sets or high temperature furnaces for biogas must be supplied with other gas sources to maintain a constant energy supply. Therefore, optimizing the operation of the existing digesters to increase the biogas production is very important.

1.5   Goal and objectives of the study

The main goal of this study is to optimize the operation performance of anaerobic reactors treating OFMSW, either by investigating the maximum organic loading rate or by co-digestion with other types of wastes for energy recovery. This goal leads to a promotion of affordable solid waste treatment technologies, which have the ability to recover valuable material from municipal solid waste, especially for the less developed countries.

In order to reach the goal, this study comprises several objectives as follows:

· to evaluate the operation performance of anaerobic reactors treating the organic fraction of municipal solid waste

· to determine the potential methane production of anaerobic degradation of biowaste and other types of waste namely foodwaste, press water and potato sludge,

· to examine the characteristics of different organic solid wastes which are potential substrates for anaerobic digestion,

· to examine the stability of the solid waste substrates if they are used as a sole substrate in anaerobic digestion, and

· to determine the maximum loading rate of the anaerobic reactors treating biowaste from municipal solid waste if co-digested with other types of wastes.

Chapter 2

ASPECTS AND DEVELOPMENTS IN ANAEROBIC DIGESTION OF ORGANIC SOLID WASTE: A LITERATURE REVIEW

The history of anaerobic digestion can be traced back 2000 years by the anaerobic digestion of animal manure in China and India (Veenstra, 2000). In modern age after the discovery of methane emissions from natural anaerobic habitats by Volta in 1776, people started to collect the natural biogas and used it as a fuel, basically for lighting. However, it took until the end of the 19th century until anaerobic digestion was applied for the treatment of wastewater and solid waste (Gijzen, 2002). The first digestion plant was reported to have been built at a leper colony in Bombay, India in 1859. Anaerobic digestion reached England in 1895, when biogas was recovered from a sewage treatment facility to fuel street lamps in Exeter (Residua, 2009). The application of anaerobic digestion with the main purpose to reduce and stabilize solid waste gained its popularity after the large-scale introduction of activated sludge systems in the mids of 20th century. Until now, anaerobic digestion of sewage sludge is still a standard practice for modern activated sludge plants.

2.1 Microbiological processes in anaerobic digestion

Anaerobic digestion is described as a series of processes involving microorganisms to break down biodegradable material in the absence of oxygen. The overall result of anaerobic digestion is a nearly complete conversion of the biodegradable organic material into methane, carbon dioxide, hydrogen sulfide, ammonia and new bacterial biomass (Veeken et al., 2000 Kelleher et al., 2002; Gallert and Winter, 2005). Buswell (1952 as cited in Gallert and Winter, 2005) proposed a generic formula describing the overall chemical reaction of the anaerobic fermentation process of organic compounds which can be used for the prediction of biogas production:

$$C_cH_hO_oN_nS_s + \frac{1}{4}(4c - h - 2o - 3n + 2s)H_2O$$
$$\rightarrow \frac{1}{8}(4c - h + 2o + 3n + 2s)CO_2 + \frac{1}{8}(4c + h - 2o - 3n - 2s)CH_4 + nNH_3 + sH_2S$$

In the anaerobic digestion process different types of bacteria degrade the organic matter successively in a multistep process and parallel reactions. The anaerobic digestion process of complex organic polymers is commonly divided into three inter-related steps: hydrolysis, fermentation (also known as acidogenesis), ß-oxidation (acetogenesis) and methanogenesis which are schematically illustrated in Figure 2.1 (modified from Stronach *et al.*, 1986; Pavlosthatis and Giraldo-Gomez, 1991).

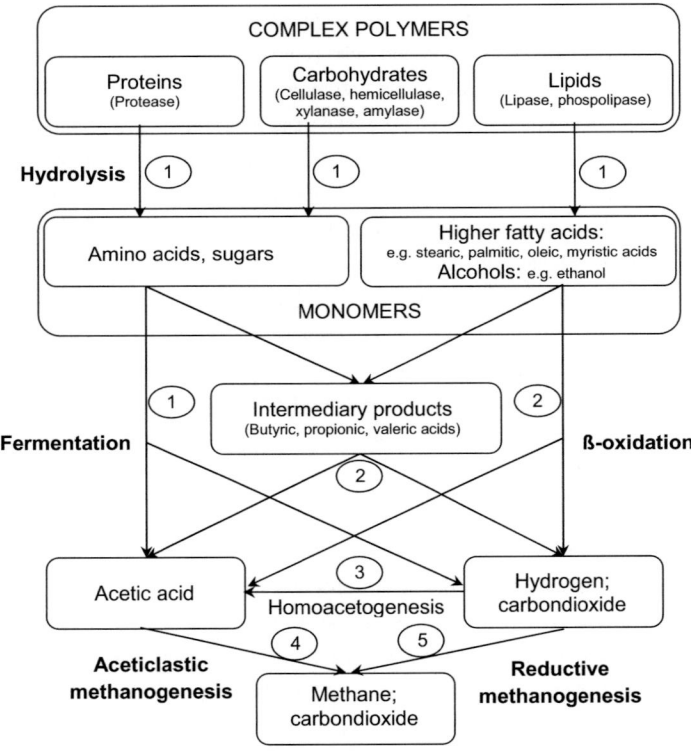

Figure 2.1 Schematic diagram of complete anaerobic digestion of complex polymers. Names in brackets indicate the enzymes excreted by hydrolytic bacteria. Numbers indicate the bacterial groups involved:
1. Fermentative bacteria
2. Hydrogen-producing acetogenic bacteria
3. Hydrogen-consuming acetogenic bacteria
4. Aceticlastic methanogenic bacteria
5. Carbon dioxide-reducing methanogenic bacteria

Hydrolysis. In the first step, complex organic polymers such as polysaccharides, proteins, and lipids (fat and grease) are hydrolyzed by extra-cellular enzymes into soluble products. The size of these soluble products must be small enough to allow their transport across the cell membrane of bacteria. Hydrolysis is a rather slow and energy-consuming process and is normally considered as the overall rate-limiting step for the complete anaerobic digestion of complex polymers (McCarty and Mosey, 1991; Pavlosthatis and Giraldo-Gomez, 1991; Gallert and Winter, 1999).

Fermentation (acidogenesis). The monomers produced from the hydrolysis process are then degraded by a large diversity of facultative anaerobes and anaerobes through many fermentative pathways. The degradation of these compounds results n the production of carbon dioxide hydrogen gas, alcohols, organic acids, some organic-nitrogen compounds, and some organic-sulfur compounds. The most important of the organic acids is acetate since it can be used directly as a substrate by methanogenic bacteria.

Acetogenesis. Acetate can be produced not only through the fermentation of soluble organic compounds but also through acetogenesis. In this step low molecular weight volatile fatty acids are converted into acetate, hydrogen gas and carbon dioxide by acetogenic bacteria. This conversion process can only be thermodynamically favoured if the partial hydrogen pressure is kept low. Thus efficient removal of the produced hydrogen gas is necessary (Pavlosthatis and Giraldo-Gomez, 1991; Veenstra, 2000, Gerardi, 2003).

Methanogenesis. Finally, methane gas is produced by methane producing bacteria. Methane is formed around 66 % from acetate by means acetate decarboxylation proceeded by acetoclastic methanogenic bacteria (*e.g. Methanosaeta* spp. and *Methanosarcina* spp.) and 34 % from carbon dioxide reduction by hydrogen, catalysed by hydrogen utilizing (hydrogenophilic) methanogenic bacteria. In particular, hydrogen utilizing methanogenic bacteria maybe responsible for the low partial pressure of hydrogen gas in anaerobic reactors, thus they create optimal conditions for acetogenic bacteria to breakdown the hydrolyzed organic compounds other than CO_2, H_2 and acetate into substrates for methanogenic bacteria (Veenstra, 2000; Metcalf & Eddy Inc., 2003). Alternatively sulphate-reducing bacteria or autotrophic acetogenic bacteria may also use hydrogen for sulphate reduction or acetate production from $CO_2 + H_2$ and thus decrease the hydrogen partial pressure.

Table 2.1 Types of bacteria involved in each step of polymeric organic material digestion

Degradation process	Bacterial group	Type of conversion	Type of bacteria
Hydrolysis	Hydrolytic bacteria	Proteins to soluble peptides and amino acids	Clostridium, Proteus vulgaris, Peptococcus, Bacteriodes, Bacillus, Vibrio
		Carbohydrates to soluble sugars	Clostridium, Acetovibrio celluliticus, Staphylococcus, Bacteriodes
		Lipids to higher fatty acids or alcohols and glycerol	Clostridium, Micrococcus, Staphylococcus
Fermentation	Acidogenic bacteria	Amino acids to fatty acids, acetate and NH_3	Lactobacillus, Escherichia, Staphylococcus, Bacillus, Pseudomonas, Desulfovibrio, Selenomonas, Sarcina, Veillonella, Streptococcus, Desulfobacter, Desulforomonas
		Sugars to intermediary fermentation products	Clostridium, Eubacterium limosum, Streptococcus
Acetogenesis	Acetogenic bacteria	Higher fatty acids or alcohols to hydrogen and acetate	Clostridium, Syntrophomonas wolfeii
		Volatile fatty acids and alcohols to acetate or hydrogen	Sytrophomonas wolfei, Sytrophomonas wolinii
Methanogenesis	Carbon dioxide-reducing methanogens	Hydrogen and carbon dioxide to methane	Methanobacterium, Methanobrevibacterium, Methanoplanus, Methanospirillum
	Aceticlastic methanogens	Acetate to methane and carbon dioxide	Methanosaeta, Methanosarcina,

Modified from: Stronach et al., 1986

2.2   Important parameters in anaerobic digestion of solid waste

Several factors can affect the performance of the anaerobic digestion, either by process enhancement or inhibition, influencing parameters such as specific growth rate, degradation rates, biogas production or substrate utilisation. This sub-chapter will briefly discuss those factors namely: pH, temperature, substrate, retention time, organic loading, mixing condition and inhibitory substances.

2.2.1   pH

The pH value of the digester content is an important indicator of the performance and the stability of an anaerobic digester. In a well-balanced anaerobic digestion process, almost all products of a metabolic stage are continuously converted into the next breaking down product without any significant accumulation of intermediary products such as different fatty acids which would cause a pH drop.

Many aspects of the complex microbial metabolism are greatly influenced by pH variations in the digester. Although acceptable enzymatic activity of acid-forming bacteria can occur at pH 5.0, methanogenesis proceeds only at a high rate when the pH is maintained in the neutral range. Most anaerobic bacteria including methane-forming bacteria function in a pH range of 6.5 to 7.5, but optimally at a pH of 6.8 to 7.6 and the rate of methane production may decrease if the pH is lower than 6.3 or higher than 7.8 (Stronach *et al.*, 1986; Lay *et al.*, 1998). Zhang *et al.* (2005) reported that an anaerobic digestion of kitchen wastes with controlled pH value at 7.0 resulted in a relatively high rate of hydrolysis and acidogenesis with about 86 % of TOC and 82 % of COD were solubilized.

Alkalinity and pH in anaerobic digestion can be adjusted using several chemicals such as sodium (bi-) carbonate, potassium (bi-) carbonate, calcium carbonate (lime), calcium hydroxide (quick lime) and sodium nitrate. Addition of any selected chemical for pH adjustment should be done slowly to prevent any adverse impact on the bacteria Because methanogenic bacteria require bicarbonate alkalinity, chemicals that directly release bicarbonate alkalinity are preferred (*e.g.* sodium bicarbonate and potassium bicarbonate are more preferred due to their desirable solubility, handling, and minimal adverse impacts). Lime may be used to increase digester pH to 6.4, and then eithebicarbonate or carbonate salts (sodium or potassium) should be used to increase the pH to the optimum range (Gerardi, 2003)

2.2.2 Temperature

Temperature is one of the major important parameters in anaerobic digestion. It determines the rate of anaerobic degradation processes particularly the rates of hydrolysis and methanogenesis. Moreover, it not only influences the metabolic activities of the microbial population but also has a significant effect on some other factors such as gas transfer rates and settling characteristics of biosolids (Stronach *et al.*, 1986 and Metcalf & Eddy Inc., 2003). Anaerobic digestion commonly applies two optimal temperature ranges: mesophilic with optimum temperature around 35 °C and thermophilic with optimum temperature around 55 °C (Mata-Alvarez, 2002, see also Figure 2.2). The biphasic curve typically is a result of insufficient adoption nd selection time by increasing the mesophilic and lowering the thermophilic temperature and not awaiting several retention times. If enough adaptation time in fed-batch and continuous cultivation is allowed, the selected populations at 30,37,45, 50 and 55 °C will produce biogas at similar rates (Figure 2.2 dotted line), with slightly lower residual fatty acid concentrations at the lower temperatures (Winter *et al.*, 1982; Temper *et al.*, 1983; Kandler *et al.*, 1983)

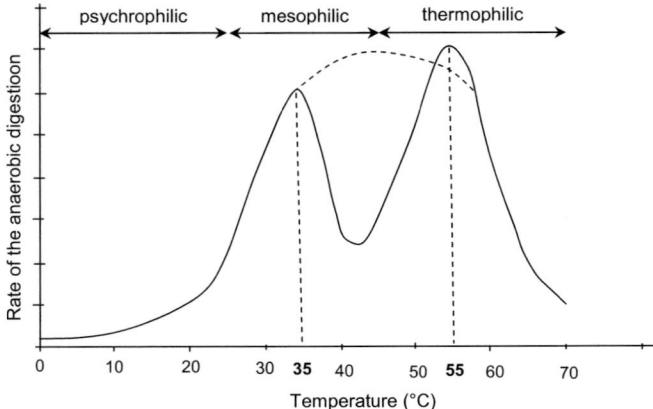

Figure 2.2 Influence of temperature on the rate of anaerobic digestion process. Optimum temperature for mesophilic around 30 – 40 °C and for thermophilic 50 – 60 °C (Source: Mata-Alvarez, 2002)

Mesophilic bacteria are supposed to be more robust and can tolerate greater changes in the environmental parameters, including temperature. Smaller digesters, poorly insulated digesters, or digesters in cold climates are susceptible for extreme temperature fluctuations thus these would be beneficial if the digester is being run in the mesophilic range to minimize system crashing. Although it requires longer retention time, the stability of the mesophilic process makes it more popular in current anaerobic digestion facilities (Zaher et al., 2007).

Thermophilic process offers faster kinetics, higher methane production rates and pathogen removal. This method, however, is more sensitive to toxic substances and changes of operation parameters (Mata-Alvarez, 2002). A study comparing the performance of thermophilic and mesophilic treating mechanically sorted municipal solid waste (Cecchi et al., 1991) found that thermophilic process yielded 100 % more methane production and better volatile solids elimination compared to mesophilic process. However, thermophilic process is sometimes considered as less attractive from the energy point of view since it requires more energy for heating (Zaher et al., 2007).

Reasonable methane yields still can be expected from anaerobic digestion at low temperatures (14 – 23 °C) if the organic loading of the digester is reduced by mean of extending the hydraulic retention (Alvarez and Lidén, 2009). The authors also reported that a relative stable operation of an anaerobic digester treating mixture of animal manure can be achieved at low temperature (18 – 25 °C) with an optimum OLR of 4 – 6 kg VS·m^{-3}·d^{-1} and a methane content of 47 – 55 % in the biogas.

The most common method for maintaining the temperature in anaerobic digester is an external heat exchanger. This method has the benefit of enabling to mix recirculating digestate with raw slurry before heating, and in seeding the raw slurry with anaerobic micro-organisms. Among three types of external heat exchangers frequently used (i.e. water bath, tubular and spiral exchangers), both tubular and spiral exchangers are mostly preferred for their countercurrent flow design and heat transfer coefficients. The hot water used in the heat exchangers is commonly produced in a boiler fueled by biogas that comes from the digester. At the start-up and/or under conditions of insufficient biogas production, an alternative fuel source such as natural gas must be provided (Appels et al., 2008).

2.2.3   Substrate characteristics

The characteristics of solid wastes determine the successful anaerobic digestion process (*e.g.* high biogas production potential and degradability). In municipal solid waste, substrate characteristics may vary due to the method of collection, weather season, cultural habits of the community *etc.* Substrate characteristics such as its composition, C/N ratio and particle size will be briefly discussed in this sub-chapter.

The degradability and biogas production potential from solid waste in an anaerobic digester are dependent on the amount of the main components: lipids, proteins, carbohydrates such as cellulose and hemicelluloses as well as lignin (Hartmann and Ahring, 2006). Among them lipids are the most significant substances in the anaerobic digestion, since the methane yield from lipids is higher than from most other organic materials. The theoretical gas yield of glyceride trioleate is, for example, 1.4 m^3 per kilogram of oil with a methane content of 70% (Hanaki *et al.*, 1981; Angelidaki *et al.*, 1990). Although organic waste with a high content of lipids is an attractive substrate for biogas production, Neves *et al.* (2008) reported that the lowest hydrolysis rate constants were obtained in the assays fed with kitchen waste that contained an excess of lipids. This was presumably due to a synergetic effect on the degradation of the other components since lipids adsorb onto solid surfaces and may delay the hydrolysis process by reducing the accessibility of enzyme attack. Lignocellulosic (cellulose and hemicelluloses which are tightly bound to the lignin) waste can be found in abundant amount in the form of garden waste, paper residue or agricultural waste. Due to the presence of lignin, lignocellulosic waste is considered to be quite resistant to anaerobic digestion and hydrolysis is the rate limiting step in the overall process. In order to improve the rate of enzyme hydrolysis and increase yields of fermentable sugars from cellulose or hemicellulose in lignocellulosic waste, several pretreatment methods such as thermal (steam or hot water), chemical (acid, lime or ammonia addition) or combination of both methods were proposed by several authors (e.g. Mosier *et al.*, 2005; Fernandes *et al.* 2009).

The composition of waste also determines the relative amounts of organic carbon and nitrogen present in the waste substrate (C/N ratio). A solid waste substrate with high C/N ratio is not suitable for bacterial growth due to deficiency of nitrogen. As a result the gas production rate and solids degradability will be low. On the other hand, if the C/N ratio is very low, the degradation process leads to ammonia accumulation which is toxic to the bacteria (Hartmann and Ahring, 2006). Kayhanian and Hardy (1995) found that a C/N ratio (based on biodegradable organic carbon and nitrogen) within the range of 25–30 is considered to be optimum for an anaerobic digester. To maintain the C/N level of the digester material at optimum levels, substrates with high C/N ratio can be co-digested with nutrient-rich organic wastes (low C/N ratio) like animal manure or foodwaste (Zaher et al., 2007).

The particle size has a significant role in anaerobic digestion of solid waste, especially during hydrolysis since a smaller particle size provides a greater area for enzymatic attack (Palmowski and Müller, 2000; Hartmann and Ahring, 2006). The increase of the average particle size in anaerobic digestion of foodwaste was reported to decrease the maximum substrate utilization rate coefficient (Kim et al., 2000). Mshandete et al. (2006) reported that by reducing the size to 2 mm, the potential methane production of sisal fiber waste will improve to more than 20 % and the total fiber degradation increased from 31% to 70% compared to the untreated fibers.

2.2.4   Hydraulic retention time and organic loading rate

The hydraulic retention time (HRT) is a measure to describe the average time that a certain substrate resides in a digester. In a digester with continuous mixing, the contents of the reactor have a relative uniform retention time. In this system, the minimum HRT is dictated by the growth rate of the slowest growing, essential microorganisms of the anaerobic bacterial community. If the HRT is shorter, the system will fail due to washout of the slowest growing microorganisms that are necessary for the anaerobic process (Zaher et al., 2007). Shortening the HRT consequently reduces the size of the digester, resulting in capital cost savings. Furthermore, a shorter HRT yields a higher biogas production rate, but less efficient degradation of organic matter (as volatile solids or COD), associated with less process stability must be anticipated.

Hartmann and Ahring (2006) compiled the reports from other researchers and found that the HRT of anaerobic digesters treating solid wastes varied from 3 to 55 days, depending on the type of waste, operational temperature, process stage(s) and configuration of the digesters. The HRT for dry anaerobic digestion ranges between 14 and 30 days and for wet anaerobic processes it can be as low as 3 days. Salminen and Rintala (2002), however, reported even a longer retention time of 50 – 100 days for a digester treating solid waste from poultry slaughterhouse. The authors also found that at a shorter retention time (13 to 25 days), the process appeared to be inhibited, as indicated by the buildup of long-chain fatty acids and a lower methane yield.

The organic loading rate (OLR) is defined as the amount of organic matter (expressed as volatile solids or COD of the feeding substrate) that must be treated by a certain volume of anaerobic digester in a certain period of time. The value of the OLR is mostly coupled with the HRT value. If the concentration of organic matter in the feedstock substrates is relatively constant, the shorter the HRT the higher value of OLR will be achieved. On the other hand, the value of the OLR will vary at the same HRT if there is a variation of organic matter concentration in the feeding substrate. The potential danger of a rapid increase in the OLR would be that the hydrolysis and acidogenic bacteria would produce intermediary products rapidly. Since the multiplication time of methanogenic bacteria is slower, they would not be able to consume the fatty acids at the same rate. The accumulation of fatty acids will lead to a pH drop and hampering the activity methanogenic bacteria, causing a system failure.

2.2.5 Mixing condition

Although there were several contradictions, researchers agreed that mixing plays an important role in anaerobic digestion of solid waste. Mixing provides an adequate contact between the incoming fresh substrate and the viable bacterial population and also prevents the thermal stratification and the formation of a surface crust/scum buildup in an anaerobic reactor (Karim *et al.*, 2005; Meroney and Colorado, 2009). Furthermore, mixing ensures that solids remain in suspension avoiding the formation of dead zones by sedimentation of sand or heavy solid particles. Mixing also enables the particle size reduction as digestion progresses and the release of produced biogas from the digester contents (Kaparaju *et al.*, 2007).

Stroot *et al.* (2001) reported that minimal mixing resulted in excellent performance of high solids digestion of OFMSW with higher gas production rates and specific gas production. Minimally mixed solid waste presumably resulted in slower hydrolysis and acidogenesis, allowing synthrophs and methanogens to consume the fermentation products and by this avoiding inhibition through accumulation of these compounds. Vigorous and continuous mixing was reported to be inhibitory at high organic loading rates probably due to the disruption of syntrophic relationships and spatial juxtapositioning.

According to Appels *et al.* (2008) mixing can be performed through several means such as mechanical mixers, recirculation of slurry (digesting sludge), or by injection of the produced biogas. Mechanical mixing systems generally use low-speed flat-blade turbines and are most suited for digesters with fixed covers. The digesting sludge is transported by the rotating impeller(s), thereby mixing the content of the digestion tank. Slurry recirculation is provided by centrifugal pumps, generally set up in an internal or external shaft tube to support vertical mixing. Slurry recirculation is performed by withdrawing the digesting sludge from the centre of the digester. The sludge is then pumped through external heat exchangers, where the digested sludge is blended with the raw sludge and heated to the desired temperature. It is then pumped back in the digestion tank through nozzles at the base of the digester or at the top to break the scum layer. The disadvantage of this method is that the flow rate in the recirculation should be very large to ensure a complete mixing (thus the energy required is high). Other disadvantages of slurry recirculation are plugging of the pumps by rags, impeller wear from grit and bearing failures. Biogas recirculation is a successful method of mixing the digester content and avoids the build-up of scum. Biogas mixing systems can be confined and unconfined. In unconfined systems, the gas is collected at the top of the digestion tank, compressed and then released through a pattern of diffusers or a series of radially placed lances suspended from the digester cover. In confined systems the gas is collected at the top, compressed and discharged through confined tubes and gas bubbles rise, creating an air-lift effect.

2.2.6 Inhibitory substances

Inhibition in anaerobic digestion process by the presence of toxic substances can occur to varying degrees, causing upset of biogas production and organic removal or even digester failure (Stronach *et al.*, 1986). These kinds of substances can be found as components of the feeding substrate (organic solid waste) or as byproducts of the metabolic activities of bacteria consortium in the digester. Previous publications on anaerobic digestion show a wide variation in the inhibition/toxicity levels for most substances. The main reason for these variations is the significant influence by microbiological mechanisms such as acclimation, antagonism, and synergism (Chen *et al.*, 2008). Acclimation is the ability of microorganism to rearrange their metabolic resources to overcome the metabolic block produced by the inhibitory or toxic substances when the concentrations of these substances are slowly increased within the environment. Antagonism is defined as a reduction of the toxic effect of one substance by the presence of another, whereas synergism is an increase in the toxic effect of one substance by the presence of another. Several substances with inhibitory/toxic potential to anaerobic digestion, such as ammonia, sulfide, light metal ions, heavy metals and organic substances, will be briefly presented in this sub-chapter.

Ammonia. Ammonia is a hydrolysis product formed during anaerobic digestion of solid waste by degradation of nitrogenous matter in the form of proteins, phospholipids, nitrogenous lipids and nucleic acid (Kayhanian, 1999; Sung and Liu, 2003). The inhibition mechanisms of ammonia are presumably due to the change of intracellular pH, the increase of maintenance energy requirement to overcome the toxic conditions, and inhibition of specific enzyme reactions (Whittmann *et al.*, 1995). In a solution, ammonium exists in the form of ammonium ion and free ammonia. Free ammonia is reported to have a more pronounced inhibition effect since it is freely membrane-permeable and may diffuse passively into the cell, causing proton imbalance and/or potassium deficiency (Eldem *et al.*, 2004; Gallert *et al.*, 1998).

Sulfide. The formation of hydrogen sulfide in anaerobic digestion is the result of the reduction of oxidized sulfur compounds and of the dissimilation of sulfur-containing amino acids such as cysteine by sulfate reducing bacteria. The reduction is performed by two major groups of SRB including incomplete oxidizers, which oxidize compounds such as lactate to acetate and CO_2 and complete oxidizers (acetoclastic SRB), which completely convert acetate to CO_2 and HCO_3^-. Both groups utilize hydrogen for sulfate reduction (Hilton and Oleszkiewicz, 1988). Inhibition caused by sulfate reduction can be differentiated into two stages. Primary inhibition is indicated by lower methane production due to competition of SRB and methanogenic bacteria to obtain common organic and inorganic substrates. Secondary inhibition results from the toxicity of sulfide to various anaerobic bacteria groups (Chen *et al.*, 2008).

Light metal ions. The light metal ions including sodium, potassium, calcium, and magnesium are commonly present in the digestate of anaerobic reactors. They may be produced by the degradation of organic matter in the feeding substrate or by chemicals addition for pH adjustment. Moderate concentrations of these ions are needed to stimulate microbial growth, however excessive amounts will slow down growth, and even higher concentrations can cause severe inhibition or toxicity. Salt toxicity is primarily associated with bacterial cells dehydration due to osmotic pressure (Chen *et al.*, 1999). Although the cations of salts in solution must always be associated with the anions, the toxic action of salts was found to be predominantly determined by the cation. The role of the anions was relatively minor and largely associated with their effect on properties such as the pH of the media. If compared on a molar concentration basis, monovalent cations, such as sodium and potassium, were less toxic than the divalent cations, such as calcium and magnesium (McCarty and McKinney, 1961).

Heavy metals. Similar with light metal ions, the presence of heavy metals in trace concentration will stimulate the growth of anaerobic digester's flora. However, unlike other toxic substances, heavy metals are not biodegradable and can accumulate to potentially toxic concentrations. An extensive study on the performance of anaerobic reactors found that heavy metal toxicity is one of the major causes of anaerobic digester upset or failure (Swanwick *et al.*, 1969 in Chen *et al.*, 2008). The toxic effect of heavy metals is attributed to their ability to inactivate a wide range of enzyme function and structures by binding of the metals with thiol (sulfhydryl) and other groups on protein molecules or by replacing naturally occurring metals in prosthetic groups of enzymes (Sanchez *et al.*, 1996; Chen *et al.*, 2008). The toxicity of heavy metals in anaerobic digestion depends upon the various chemical forms which the metals may assume under anaerobic conditions at the temperature and pH value in the digester. For instance, heavy metals in the precipitated form have little toxic effect on the biological system (Angelidaki and Westermann, 1983).

Organic substances. Many organic compounds were reported to have a inhibitory potential to anaerobic digestion processes. The accumulation of hydrophobic organic pollutants in bacterial membranes causes the membrane to swell and leak, disrupting ion gradients and eventually causing the breaking of cellular membranes (Heipieper *et al.*, 1994; Sikkema *et al.*, 1994 in Chen *et al.*, 2008). The toxicity concentration of organic compounds ranges vary widely and is affected by many parameters, including toxicant concentration, biomass concentration, toxicant exposure time, cell age, feeding pattern, acclimation and temperature (Yang and Speece, 1986). Several important organic substances which are inhibitory to anaerobic digestion are: chlorophenols, halogenated aliphatic, nitrogen-substituted aromatic, long-chain fatty acids and lignins/lignin related compounds.

Several strategies to minimize the effect of inhibitory substances can be summarized as follows (Angelidaki and Ahring, 1993; Wittmann *et al.*, 1995; Kayhanian, 1999; Bashir and Matin, 2004; Angelidaki *et al.*, 2006; Zaher *et al.*, 2007):

a. Removal of potential inhibitory/toxic substances from the feeding substrate.
b. Dilution of the feeding substrate in order to reduce the concentration of inhibitory substances below the threshold.
c. Addition of chemicals to precipitate or insolubilize the inhibitory substances.
d. Change of the chemical form of inhibitory substances through pH control.
e. Addition of material that is antagonistic to the inhibitory substances in order to counteract the inhibitory effect.

2.3 Types of anaerobic reactors for organic solid wastes

Typically anaerobic reactors or processes of solid waste can be distinguished into several types, mostly according to the feeding mode (continuous mode: single stage, two stages and batch mode) and the moisture content of the substrate (wet or dry digestion). Furthermore with those basic types, the anaerobic reactors can be arranged according to the digestion process temperature (mesophilic or thermophilic) and the shape of the reactors (vertical or horizontal).

2.3.1 Wet and dry anaerobic digestion:

Anaerobic digestion processes can be termed as "wet" and "dry" digestions depending on the total solids concentration of the feed substrate. Anaerobic digestion is defined as a wet process if the total solids concentration of the substrate is less than 15% and as a dry process if the concentration reaches 20 – 40% (Lissens *et al.*, 2001).

In wet digestion processes, the solid waste has to be conditioned to the appropriate solids concentration by adding process water either by recirculation of the liquid effluent fraction, or by co-digestion with a more liquid waste. The latter is an attractive method to combine several waste streams like sewage sludge or manure and OFMSW (Luning *et al.*, 2003, Hartmann and Ahring, 2006). Reactors used in wet digestion processes generally are referred to as continuous stirred tank reactors (CSTR), with application of mechanical mixers or a combination of mechanical mixing and biogas injection (Banks and Stentiford, 2007). The application of a wet digestion process offers several advantages such as dilution of inhibitory substances by process water and requirement of less sophisticated mechanical equipments. However, disadvantages, such as complicated pre-treatment, high consumption of water and energy for heating and the reduction of working volume due to sedimentation of inert materials have to be taken into account (Vandevivere et al., 2002; Banks and Stentiford, 2007).

The reactors used in dry anaerobic digestion processes generally do not apply mechanical mixers and may use biogas injection to perform mixing of the digester content (Luning et al., 2003). However, using this technique, complete mixing of the digestate is almost impossible; thus, the ideal contact of microorganisms and substrate cannot be guaranteed. As a consequence, individual processes may run in different parts of the reactor, which limits an optimal co-operation of the microbial groups involved in the digestion process (Hartmann and Ahring, 2006). Thus, the digesters used in dry anaerobic digestion can be considered as plug flow reactors (Luning et al., 2003). Dry anaerobic digestion offers less complicated pre-treatments and higher loading rate (10 kg $VS \cdot m^{-3} \cdot d^{-1}$ or more). However, the systems require more sophisticated mechanical equipments (Lissens et al., 2001) and less possibility to dilute the inhibitory substances (Vandevivere et al., 2002).

In general, both anaerobic digestion processes can be considered a proven technology for the treatment of organic solid waste. Luning et al., (2003) reported that biogas production figures of the wet digestion process (Waasa process) and the dry digestion process (Valorga process) were identical. The wet process produced more wastewater; however, this was compensated by a smaller amount of digestate to be disposed of and the separation of inert materials suitable for recycling. De Baere and Mattheews (2008) reported that although the applications of both systems have continued to increase in total capacity, dry digestion systems have been dominant since the beginning of the 1990's. An increase of wet systems was observed between 2000 and 2005 as a number of full-scale wet plants were operated, while more dry fermentation plants were being installed since 2005. In 2008, dry anaerobic digestion provided almost 54% of the capacity while the rest applied wet anaerobic digestion.

2.3.2   Batch and continuous feeding systems

Two feeding modes are generally used in anaerobic digestion of solid waste: the batch system and the continuous system. In the batch system, digesters are filled once with fresh feedstock, with or without addition of inocula, and sealed for the complete retention time, after which it is opened and the effluent removed. In the continuous system, fresh feedstock continuously enters the digester and an equal amount of digested material is removed.

Batch systems are often considered as "accelerated landfill boxes", although in fact they achieve much higher biogas production rates than that observed in landfills, because of two basic features. The first feature is that the continuous recirculation of leachate not only allows the dispersion of inoculants, nutrients, and acids, but also improves the mixing condition. The second is that batch system is run at higher temperatures than that normally observed in landfills. One technical shortcoming of batch system is the risk of blockage of the leaching process caused by clogging of the perforated floor. This problem is alleviated by mixing the feedstock with bulking material (*e.g.* wood chips) and by limiting the thickness of the fermenting wastes in order to limit compaction (Vandevivere *et al.*, 2003). Although batch systems have not succeeded in taking a substantial market share, especially in more developed countries, the system is attractive to developing countries. The reason is that the process offers several advantages as it does not require fine shredding of waste, sophisticated mixing or agitation equipments, or expensive, high-pressure vessels, which consequently lower the investment costs (Ouedraogo, 1999 in Vandevivere *et al.*, 2002; Koppar and Pullammanappallil, 2008).

As has been discussed previously, the anaerobic digestion of organic wastes is accomplished by a series of biochemical processes. These processes can be separated into two main stages: the first stage where hydrolysis, acidification and liquefaction take place and the second stage where acetate, hydrogen and carbon dioxide are converted into methane. Concerning these processes, the continuous system can be further divided to one-stage and two/multi-stage system. (Lissens *et al.*, 2001; Vandevivere *et al.*, 2002).

In one-stage systems, all biochemical processes take place simultaneously in a single reactor. The major drawback of single-stage digester systems is that these processes are required to proceed under the same operating conditions despite differences in growth rates and optimal pH of the microbial groups involved in each step. This is the reason why single-stage systems are more easily to upset compared to multi-stage systems. This disadvantage is substantial especially in the case of substrates where degradation is limited by methanogenesis rather than by hydrolysis, e.g. cellulose-poor kitchen wastes. These wastes, being very rapidly acidified, tend to inhibit the methanogenesis when the feedstock is not adequately mixed, buffered and dosed (Vandevivere et al., 2002; Gerardi, 2003).

The concept of two/multi-stages systems offers optimization of the digestion conditions by providing separate reactors for each step. The conditions in the first reactor are adjusted to favor the growth of organisms that are capable of breaking down biopolymers and releasing fatty acids (hydrolysis/acidification). The product of the first reactor is then passed to the second reactor, where methanogenesis occurs (Schober et al., 1999; de Baere, 2000). The potential drawback of two/multi-stages systems is the decrease of biogas yield due to solid particles removal from the feedstock to the second stage (Vandevivere et al., 2002).

Although theoretically two/multi-stage systems have the advantage in the increase of both rate of conversion and extent of utilization of polymeric biomass material, the full-scale application is very moderate. The decision makers and industrialists prefer one-stage systems because they have simpler designs, suffer less frequent technical failures and have smaller investment costs. Moreover, for most organic waste, the biological performance of one-stage systems is as high as that of two-stage systems if the reactor is well designed and operating conditions are carefully chosen (de Baere 2000; Vandevivere et al., 2002). Therefore, in 2008 more than 90 % of the full-scale plants in Europe for anaerobic digestion of biowastes rely on one-stage systems and these are approximately evenly split between 'wet' and 'dry' operating conditions (de Baere and Mattheews, 2008).

2.3.3   Commercial processes of anaerobic digestion of organic solid waste

Stimulated by the increasing demand of anaerobic digester for organic solid wastes several commercial anaerobic digester plant designs have been developed over the past two decades. Especially in European countries, there are many different processes available on the market. The processes are patented according to several basic characteristics as previously discussed (batch or continuous feeding, number of stages, total solids content of waste and operating temperature). Mixing methods (gas injection or mechanical stirrers), reactor type (vertical or horizontal, rectangular or cylindrical) and process flow (completely mixed or plug-flow) are also parameters to obtain patent rights. Figure 2.3 presents the available anaerobic digestion technology for solid waste treatment especially in the European market.

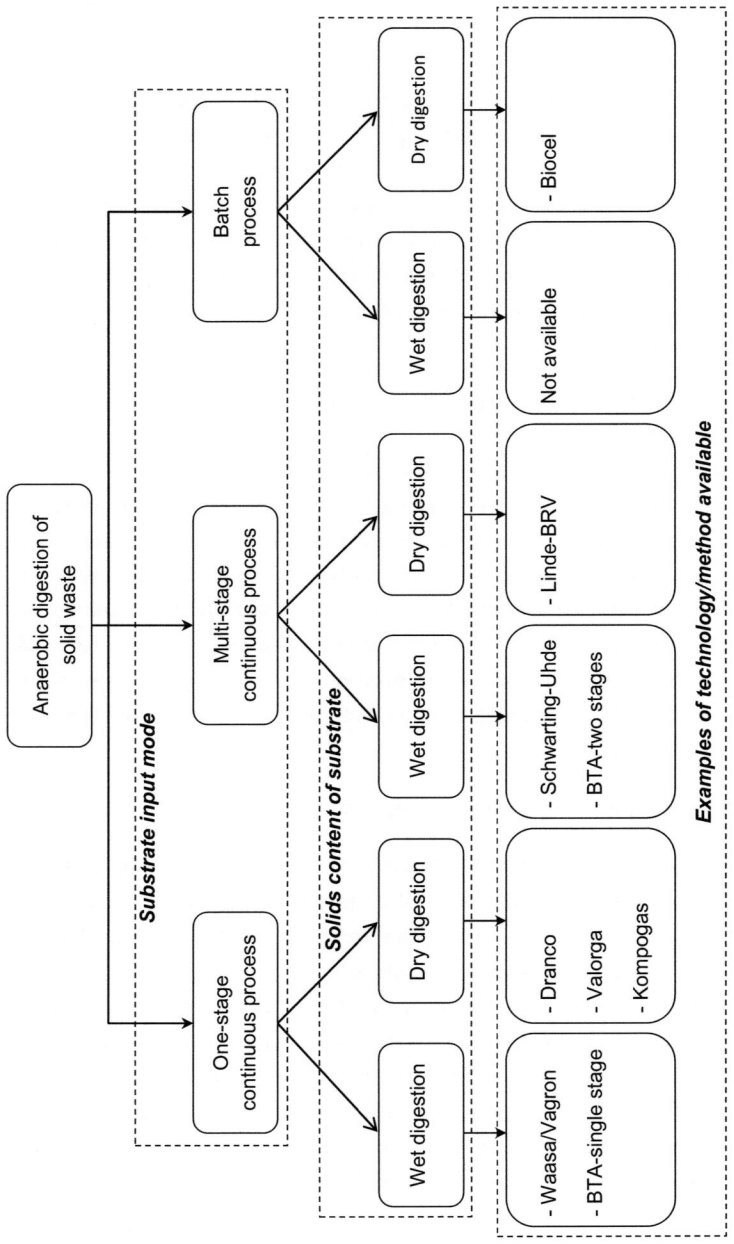

Figure 2.3 Various anaerobic digestion methods available in the market

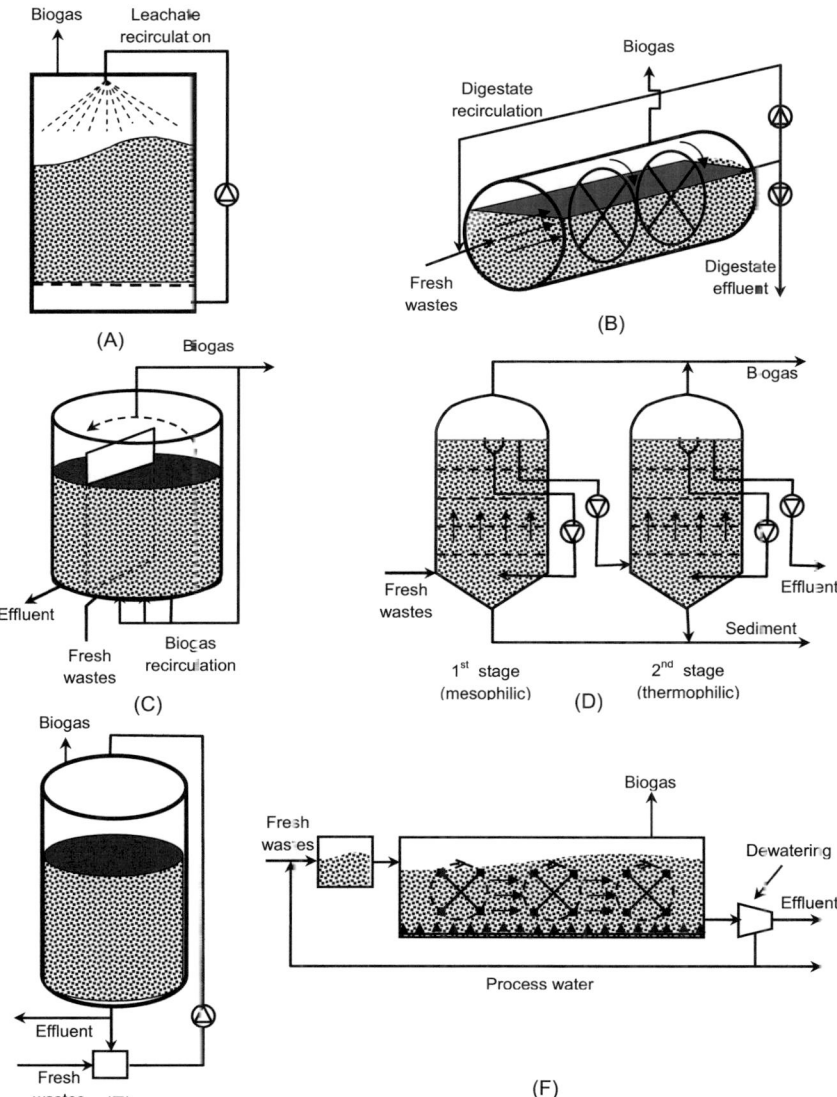

Figure 2.4 Simplified diagram of different designs of anaerobic digesters. (A) BIOCEL, (B) KOMPOGAS, (C) Valorga, (D) Schwarting-Uhde, (E) DRANCO and (F) Linde-BRV.

Several patented processes have been successfully proven their reliable performance in full-scale plants. More detailed concepts of processes namely BIOCEL (batch system), DRANCO, Valorga, KOMPOGAS (one-stage dry system), Waasa, BTA (one-stage wet system), Schwarting-Uhde (two-stage wet system) and Linde-BRV (two stage dry system) are briefly presented in this sub-chapter.

BIOCEL. The system is based on a batch-wise dry anaerobic digestion. The total solids concentration of organic solid wastes as feeding substrate is maintained at 30–40% dry matter (w/w). The process is accomplished in several rectangular concrete digesters at mesophilic temperature. The floors of the digesters are perforated and equipped with a chamber below for leachate collection. Prior to feeding, fresh biowaste substrate and inocula (digestate from previous feeding) are mixed then loaded to the digester by shovels. After the loading is finished, the digesters are closed with air tight doors. In order to control the odor emission; the system is housed in a closed building that is kept at a slight under-pressure. The temperature is controlled at 35–40ºC by spraying leachate, which is pre-heated by a heat exchanger, from nozzles on top of the digesters. Typical retention time in this process is reported to be 15 – 21 days (ten Brummeler, 2000). A full-scale BIOCEL plant is reported to have successfully treated vegetable, garden and fruit wastes with the capacity of 35,000 tons/year. Approximately 310 kg of high-quality compost, 455 kg of water, 100 kg of sand, 90 kg of biogas with an average methane content of 58% and 45 kg of inert waste are produced from each ton of waste processed (CADDET, 2000).

DRANCO. The DRANCO (dry anaerobic composting) process employs a one-stage anaerobic digestion system, which is followed by a short aerobic maturation phase. Although mostly operated under thermophilic temperature (reportedly to be 50-55 °C), mesophilic operation (35-40 °C) can also be applied for specific waste streams (de Baere, 2008). The DRANCO process is typically a vertical plug-flow reactor. The digester is fed from the top of the reactor and the digested slurry is removed from the bottom at the same time. Usually one part of the digested slurry is used as inoculum and mixed with six to eight part of fresh substrate. A small amount of steam is introduced to the mixture in order to maintain the temperature. The pre-heated mixture is then pumped to the top of the reactor through feeding tubes. There are no mixing devices needed in the reactor other than the natural downward movement of the waste caused by fresh feeding and digestate withdrawal (Vandevivere *et al.*, 2002; Edelmann and Engeli, 2005; de Baere, 2008). The rest of the digested slurry is dewatered and the solid residue from the process is then stabilized and sanitized aerobically during a period of approximately two weeks. The DRANCO process is considered to be effective for treatment of solid wastes with 20-50 % TS. The typical retention time is 15 to 30 days, and the biogas yield ranges between 100 and 200 m^3/ton of input waste (Nichols, 2004).

Valorga. The Valorga system is a one-stage dry anaerobic digestion process which uses a vertical cylindrical reactor which can be operated at both, mesophilic and thermophilic temperature. In order to obtain a horizontal plug-flow process, the digester is equipped with a vertical median partition wall on approximately 2/3 of their diameter The biowaste substrate is fed through a port placed on one side of the partition wal and the digestate withdrawal port is placed on the other side. The vertical mixing is performed by internally recirculated high-pressure biogas injection every 15 minutes. The pre-treatments prior to feeding include: dry ballistic separation to remove the heavy fraction and other contaminants, crushing of biowaste to obtain particle size < 80 mm, adjustment of solids content to 25 -32 % by mixing with process water, and pre-heating by steam injection (Fruteau de Laclos *et al.*, 1997; Karagiannidis and Perkoulidis, 2009). The retention time of this system is typically 18 – 25 days at mesophilic temperatures with a biogas yield of 80 to 160 $m^3 \cdot ton^{-1}$ of feedstock, depending on the type of solid waste (Nichols, 2004). One technical drawback of the system design is that gas injection ports are easily clogged when treating relative wet (< 20 % TS) feed stock (Vandevivere *et al.*, 2002). Edelmann and Engeli (2005) reported that the operation of a thermophilic Valorga digester in Switzerland was stopped for a relatively long time because of large quantities of sediments (sand, gravel *etc.*) in the base of the digester, hampering the function of the mixing equipment and reducing the active volume of the digester significantly.

KOMPOGAS. The KOMPOGAS system is a one-stage dry anaerobic digestion process. The fermentation process takes place in a horizontal plug-flow reactor at thermophilic temperature (typically 55-60 °C). The reactor is equipped by slowly rotating and intermittently acting impellers to ensure mixing and help the re-suspension of heavier materials. Prior to feeding, the solid waste is mechanical pre-treated in order to remove the impurities and reduce the size of the substrate (KOMPOGAS, 2007). A total solids content adjustment by addition of process water is done to have a TS concentration to around 23 to 28 %. If the TS values are lower than this range, heavy particles such as sand and glass tend to sink and accumulate inside the reactor while higher values can cause excessive resistance to the flow (Chavez-Vazquez and Bagley, 2002). The retention time of the system ranged from 15 – 20 days. Due to mechanical constraints, the volume of the KOMPOGAS reactor is limited. If the solid waste generation is relatively high, the capacity of the plant can be facilitated by installing several reactors in parallel, each with a capacity of either 15,000 or 25,000 tons/year (Nichols, 2004). The KOMPOGAS system is reported to run very stable, however, it has to be stressed that it is important to feed an appropriate mixture of wastes. A KOMPOGAS plant which was run exclusively with protein-rich food wastes first experienced an inhibition due to high ammonia concentrations (Edelmann and Engeli, 2005). Nishio and Nakashimada (2007) reported that three types of waste (*i.e.,* garbage and rejects from hotels, yard waste, and old paper) were mixed at various ratios to control the C/N ratio before feeding to the KOMPOGAS plant. The plant ran at stable operation for at least two years and generated biogas at a rate of about 820 m^3/ton of VS.

Waasa. The Waasa process is a wet, one-stage anaerobic digestion system and is operated at both, mesophilic and termophilic temperatures. This completely mixed process is maintained in a vertical reactor which is subdivided internally to create a pre-digestion chamber by which the possibility of short-circuiting should be prevented. A relatively complex pre-treatment including mechanical sorting and waste washing has to be done prior to feeding. The sorting facility produces by-products such as relatively high-calorie RDF (Refuse-Derived Fuel) stream, ferrous/non-ferrous metal fractions, paper and plastic fraction. The washing process comprises a wet separation process that removes coarse inert materials and sand from the organic fraction. Process water is added to fresh substrate to the desired concentration of total solids (10-15% TS). The slurry is mixed with small amount of inocula, pre-heated with steam injection and pumped to the pre-chamber which is operated in a plug-flow mode with retention times of one or two days before digestion in the main reactor. The mixing in the digester is performed by mechanical impellers and injection of a portion of the biogas into the bottom of the digester tank (Williams *et al.*, 2003). Nichols (2004) reported a full-scale Waasa process plant which was run at both temperatures parallelly. The thermophilic process required a retention time of 10 days compared to 20 days in the mesophilic process. A modified Waasa process (Vagron) treating the mechanically separated organic fraction of municipal solid waste in Groningen, the Netherlands was reported to reach a stable operation at an OLR of 7.7 kg VS $\cdot m^{-3} \cdot d^{-1}$ (Luning *et al.*, 2003). The biogas production was reported within the range of 100-150 m^3/ton of feedstock with

20-30% internal biogas consumption for the pre-heating of the feeding substrate. The volume reduction reached approximately 60%, and the weight reduction was about 50-60% (Williams *et al.*, 2003).

BTA. The BTA process consists of two major steps: the hydro-mechanical pre-treatment and the anaerobic digestion processes. During the hydro-mechanical pre-treatment the solids are diluted in hydropulpers with recirculated process water in order to obtain a maximum solids content of 10%. The light impurities like plastics, foils, textiles, wood *etc* as well as heavy impurities like stone, batteries, metals *etc* are removed by means of a rake and a heavy fraction trap. This process results in a thick, pumpable suspension that is fed to the digester. The grit removal system can be optionally added in order to separate the remaining finest matter like sand, little stones and glass splinters. Although commonly applied as single-stage system, BTA also offers a multi-stages system depending on the size of the plant. Single-stage systems are mainly for relatively small, decentralized waste management units whereas multi-stages systems are mainly for plants with capacities of more than 50,000 tons/year. The temperature in BTA process is maintained in the mesophilic range, normally at 35 °C and the digester is considered as a completely mixed reactor. Mixing is performed by biogas injection. The digestion residue is dewatered by a decanter centrifuge and generally sent to aerobic post-treatment. The water demand of the process is met by recirculating the process water. Depending upon the waste composition and local requirements, excess process water is sent to the sewage system, or will be additionally treated on-site before it can be discharged. The generated biogas can be recovered for use in gas engines or co-heat and power (CHP) stations. Depending on the waste composition, the gas yield ranges between 80 and 120 m^3/ton of biowaste (Kübler *et al.*, 2000; Chavez-Vazquez and Bagley, 2002; Nichols, 2004; Haines, 2008).

Schwarting-Uhde. The Schwarting-Uhde process adopts a two-stage wet anaerobic digestion process which is performed in a series of two vertical plug-flow reactors. The first reactor is operated at mesophilic temperature for hydrolysis and acidification processes while the second reactor is operated at thermophilic temperature for methanogenesis. The source-sorted biowaste is shredded to reduce the particle size and diluted to a TS concentration of around 12 %. The slurry is pre-heated to the intended temperature by heat exchangers and then pumped through a series of perforated plates placed within the reactor, which is employed to ensure the uniformity of upward movement and to maintain plug-flow conditions. Mechanical stirrers are not needed in for mixing purposes. An adequate mixing is obtained by raising and lowering the column of liquid in the tank, thus creating turbulence at the perforated plates via time-controlled impulse pumps. The retention time in both reactors is about 5 to 6 days making an overall retention time of 10 to 12 days. Biogas is collected at the top of the digesters, whereas settled heavy solids, which accumulate at the bottom of the reactors, are frequently removed via screw pumps. This process design offers an advantage in decreasing the potential formation of a thick floating scum layer which is commonly plaguing wet anaerobic digestion. However, due to the high risk of perforated plates clogging, the Schwarting-Uhde process is only suitable to treat relatively clean highly biodegradable biowastes (Lissens, *et al.*, 2001; Vandevivere *et al.*, 2002). A full-scale Schwarting–Uhde plant was reported to have stable operation at an OLR of up to 6 kg VS·m^{-3} ·d^{-1} (Thrösch and Niemann, 1999 in Trzcinski and Stuckey, 2009). A successful solids elimination of 55 – 60 % was reported to be achieved by a Schwarting-Uhde plant treating sludge from a wastewater treatment plant (EC, 1995).

Linde-BRV. The Linde-BRV process can be considered as two-stage dry anaerobic digestion. After pre-treatment to reduce the particle size and to remove impurities, the solids concentration of source-separated biowastes is adjusted to 34 %. The slurry is then pre-digested in an aerobic upstream stage where the organic materials are partially hydrolyzed (Vandevivere *et al.*, 2002). After 2 days of retention time, the pre-digested slurry is pumped to a rectangular shaped concrete digester in horizontal plug-flow mode. The mixing is accomplished by several agitators of transverse paddles. The horizontal plug-flow movement is ensured by a walking floor installed on the bottom of the reactor which also functions to transport the sediments to the digester's discharging end (Nichols, 2004; Zaher *et al.*, 2007). The process is commonly kept at thermophilic temperature although modification to mesophilic is also possible. Some of the heating is done outside the digester with a short heat exchanger, but primarily heating occurs within the digester walls using a heat exchanger. In the termophilic process, the retention time is reported about 21-25 days with an OLR of 8 kg VS ·m^{-3} ·d^{-1} (Vandevivere, 2002; Zaher *et al.*, 2007).

2.4   Process improvement and current state

Although it is quite difficult to compare due to experimental set-ups and/or materials, in the last 10 years, anaerobic digestion of solid waste has been gaining more attention from scientists and industrialists. Many researches and reports have been conducted regarding almost every aspect of anaerobic digestion of solid waste which are useful for process improvement or to actualize a more robust reactor design. Some authors focused on the kinetics of anaerobic biodegradation of complex waste such as OFMSW which is considered as a key issue for the understanding of the process and for the design of treatment units. Mata-Alvarez *et al.* (2000), for instance, compiled the first order kinetic constant values for hydrolysis (which is considered as rate limiting step in anaerobic digestion of solid waste) of different materials. Other papers (refer to sub-chapter 2.2 and 2.3) reported the performance of different reactor configurations (one-stage or multi-stage, dry or wet) and effects of inhibition substances, as well as effects of basic parameters such as pH, temperature, mixing, *etc.* This sub-chapter will briefly discuss some aspects which have not been discussed previously namely: pre-treatment for process enhancement, co-digestion OFMSW with other types of waste, and current state application of anaerobic digestion of solid waste technologies.

2.4.1   Pre-treatments for process enhancement

Due to the substrate characteristics, hydrolysis is considered as the rate limiting step in anaerobic digestion of OFMSW. Therefore, many researches were focused on the process in order to improve degradation rates and biogas yields. According to several reports, hydrolysis improvement can be achieved through proper pre-treatments which have obvious links to the increase of biogas yields. Pre-treatment methods for OFMSW can be biological, mechanical or physico-chemical (Delgenès *et al.*, 2003).

Biological pre-treatment can be achieved by the means of for example aerobic pre-composting methods which show positive improvement of methane yields and solids reduction (Capela *et al.*, 1999 in Mata-Alvarez *et al.*, 2000). Miah *et al.* (2005) reported that addition of aerobic thermophilic sludge improves the biogas production and solids reduction, presumably that thermophilic aerobic bacteria secrete external enzymes which dissolve particulate organic matters more actively.

Mechanical pre-treatment is commonly aimed to reduce particle size. Comminution to reduce the size of waste particles provides several advantages including the increase of dissolved compounds due to cell rupture, exposition of surface areas which were previously inaccessible for microbial degradation and alteration of the sample structure such as the lignocelluloses arrangements (Palmowski and Müller, 2003).

Chemical pre-treatment can be accomplished by alkaline pre-treatment. The chemical treatment of the fibres with NaOH, NH_4OH or a combination led to an increased methane potential (Mata-Alvarez et al., 2000). The same improvement was also reported when a pre-treatment by addition of lime was done (López-Torres and Espinosa- Lloréns, 2008).

2.4.2 Co-digestion of OFMSW with other types of waste

Co-digestion of OFMSW with other types of waste is an interesting alternative to improve biogas production, to obtain a more stable process and to achieve a better handling of waste. However, some possible disadvantages (e.g transport costs of co-substrate, additional pre-treatment facilities and the problems arising from the harmonization of the waste generators) have to be taken into account (Mata-Alvarez et al., 2003). The key factor of successful co-digestion is that the balance of macro and micro nutrients can be assured by co-substrate.

A good co-substrate should fulfil several requirements, such as: i) its concentration of organic substances should be comparable with biowaste, so that addition will not significantly affect the hydraulic retention time, ii) it should consist of easily degradable organics with a high biogas production potential, iii) it may not contain any dangerous or poisonous substances, which hinder anaerobic digestion or composting, iv) it should have a content of macro and micro nutrients which have possibility to improve the characteristics of main substrate, v) it must be available in sufficient quantities at a reasonable price and should be storable and vi) it should be pumpable without danger of clogging, thus allowing safe automatic feeding.

Various types of solid waste streams such as sewage sludge, animal manure and organic industrial waste have been proposed as co-substrate for anaerobic digestion of OFMSW. Reports on co-digestion of the organic fraction of municipal solid waste with any other waste streams, such as energy crops (Nordberg and Edström, 2005), market residues (Gallert et al., 2003), sewage sludge (Hartmann et al., 2003) and manure (Hartmann and Ahring, 2005) are existing. Sewage sludge is available in abundant quantity in line with the presence of wastewater treatment plants. Co-digestion with sewage sludge will improve the characteristics of OFMSW including its content of micro and macro nutrients, lead to a better C/N ratio and facilitate the adjustment of moisture content. The optimal mixture of OFMSW and sewage sludge depends on the specific waste characteristics and the system used in the digestion process. For wet anaerobic digestion, the best performance (in term of biogas production and VS reduction) can be achieved when the mixture of OFMSW and sewage sludge is within the range of 80:20 on TS basis or 25:75 on volume basis (Hartmann et al., 2003).

It has been discussed previously that animal manure has being used as a substrate for anaerobic digestion since more than 2000 years ago. The advantages of using animal manure as co-substrate in anaerobic digestion of OFMSW are: its abundant availability and its high buffer capacity mainly due to its ammonia content. Furthermore, animal manure has low TS content which can be used to adjust the moisture of OFMSW and wide variety of nutrients which are necessary for optimal bacterial growth. Macias-Corral et al. (2008) reported that co-digestion of OFMSW and cow manure resulted in higher methane gas yields and promoted synergistic effects resulting in higher mass conversion and lower weight and volume of digested waste.

Full-scale applications of solid waste co-digestion have been reported by several authors. Angelidaki and Ellegaard (2003) reported that in 2001, Denmark had already 22 large-scale centralized biogas plants operated under co-digestion mode and treating mainly manure together with other organic waste such as industrial organic wastes source sorted household waste, and sewage sludge. Positive results including the increase of energy production and degradation efficiency from a full-scale co-digestion of sewage sludge and OFMSW in Velenje, Slovenia were also reported (Zupančič et al., 2008). Despite the positive results from laboratory experiments and/or full-scale experience, in Europe co-digestion is less applied than it was expected. It is quite common that an organic solid co-substrate is added to manure digesters in small amounts, but often these co-substrates are high-energy yielding industrial sludge and only quite exceptionally, solid waste from households or market waste is added. Among the biogas plants identified, only about 9.7 % of the organic solid waste treated was done by means of co-digestion, mostly with liquid manure. The percentage of installed co-digestion plants has dropped from 23% in the period 1990–1995 to 5% in the period 2006–2010. However, due to the high prices for agricultural crops, many energy crop digestion plants are looking for organic waste feedstock (de Baere, 2008).

2.4.3   Economical aspects and current state application

In industrial terms, anaerobic digestion of solid waste can be considered as a mature technology. A wide range of technologies and researches are available together with holistic methods of decision support system. Many comparison or feasibility studies were carried out in order to define the optimum strategy of municipal solid waste management.

Murphy and McKeogh (2004) conducted a study comparing four technologies which produce energy from municipal solid waste (MSW): incineration, gasification, generation of biogas and utilization in a CHP plant, generation of biogas and conversion to transport fuel. The authors concluded that biogas technologies require significantly less investment costs than the thermal conversion technologies (incineration and gasification) and also have smaller gate fees. However, for biogas conversion to transport fuel, a shortcoming of only 50 % of biogas produced available for CH_4 enrichment has to be taken into account. In term of operating parameters, Hartmann and Ahring (2006) performed an extended cost-benefit calculation of the anaerobic digestion of OFMSW and found that the highest benefit can be achieved in an operation with lower OLR and longer HRT rather than when only the biogas production rate is regarded.

De Baere (2008) reported that initially in 1990 there were only three anaerobic digestion plants in Europe (each treated more than 3,000 tons/year) with a total capacity of 87,000 tons/year. Since then, the capacity has greatly increased. However, the increase in additional digestion capacity was initially rapid but has leveled off during the past five years. Schu and Schu (2007) reported that many suppliers of anaerobic digestion technologies in the market over the last ten years are now insolvent or no longer active in anaerobic digestion because of the high-risk associated with digestion of waste. The current situation is that there will be 171 plants with a total installed capacity of 5,204,000 tons/year by the end of 2010 spread over 17 European countries (de Baere, 2008).

Chapter 3

MATERIALS AND METHODS

3.1 Organic solid wastes and anaerobic sludge inocula

Several organic solid wastes were analyzed in this study in order to examine the possibility of their use as a substrate in anaerobic digestion for energy recovery. These substrates were: source-sorted OFMSW (later called biowaste) as the main substrate, pressing leachate from OFMSW composting plant (press water) as the main and co-substrate, source-sorted foodwaste (foodwaste) as co-substrate, and sludge from a potato industry wastewater treatment plant (potato sludge) as co-substrate.

3.1.1 Biowaste

The biowaste suspension used in this study was the same as that which was prepared from source-sorted domestic biowaste and that was treated in the biowaste treatment plant of Karlsruhe/Durlach. This full-scale biowaste treatment plant applies the BTA/MAT process for the preparation of the biowaste suspension. The digester has a total volume of 1,300 m^3 and a working volume of 1,000 m^3. More than 11,000 tons source-sorted OFMSW per year are processed and digested (the plant was actually sized for 8,000 tons per year). The operation of this full-scale methane reactor is the basic reference of this study. The separately collected biowaste fraction is squeezed in a mill to tear apart plastic bags and then defibered in the BTA/MAT hydropulper after addition of two parts of process water (supernatant of centrifuged digester effluent + rain water). The addition of ~12 m^3 process water to 6 tons of biowaste for hydropulping results in a moisture content of more than 90% in order to perform a wet anaerobic digestion. Heavy materials (cans, stones, ceramics, knifes, forks and spoons, *etc.*) sediment at the bottom and are withdrawn from the bottom while light materials (mostly plastics) form a scum layer at the top of the hydropulper during and after hydropulping and is scimmed of. Fine sand separation is achieved by two hydrocyclones during interim storage. The different steps involved in the biowaste treatment plant are depicted in Figure 3.1. The suspension samples for the laboratory experiments were collected after the hydro-pulper and light and heavy material removal, before entering the full-scale digester. The samples were collected monthly from the interim storage tank and stored in a refrigerator until it was used.

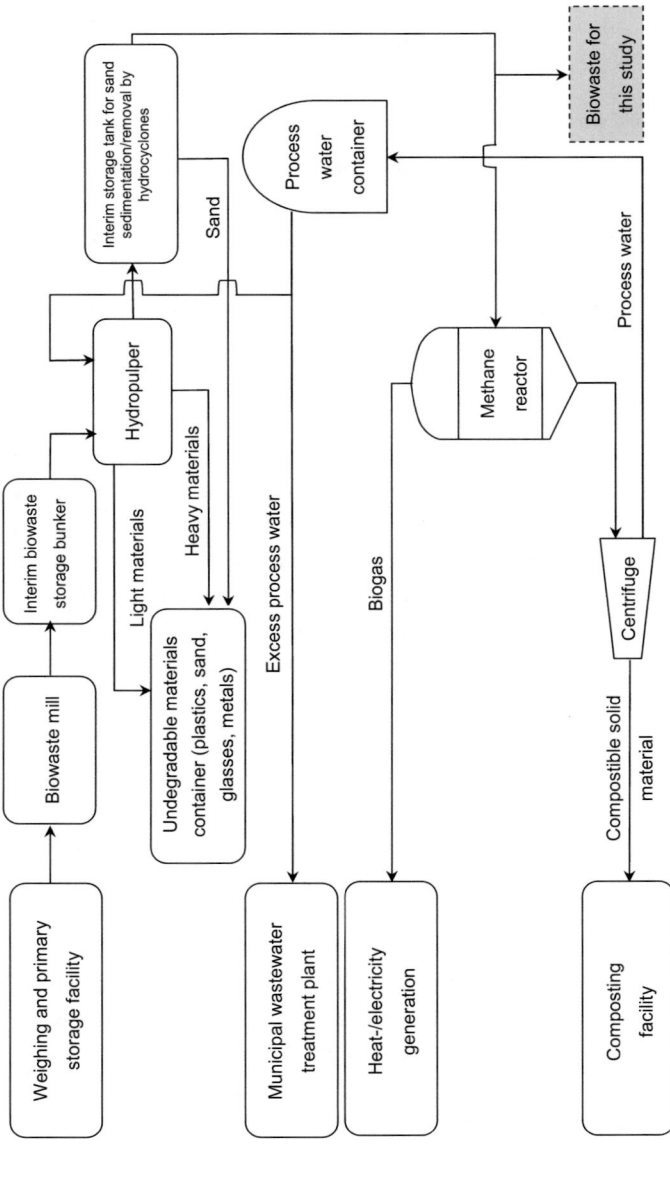

Figure 3.1 Schematic diagram of processes involved in an anaerobic digestion of biowaste (in this case: anaerobic digester in Karlsruhe–Durlach)

3.1.2 Foodwaste

Foodwaste can be obtained in sufficient quantity as a sanitized and homogeneous suspension from several private or municipal companies which collect food residues from hotels and restaurants, hospitals, university canteens, supermarkets and catering companies. In this study, the foodwaste was delivered by *Abfallwirtschaft und Stadtreinigung Freiburg GmbH*. In this company, foodwaste is grinded, homogenized and then autoclaved according to legal requirements. Homogeneous portions of 1 L samples were frozen until it was used. The typical treatment steps involved in foodwaste processing in the company are depicted in Figure 3.2.

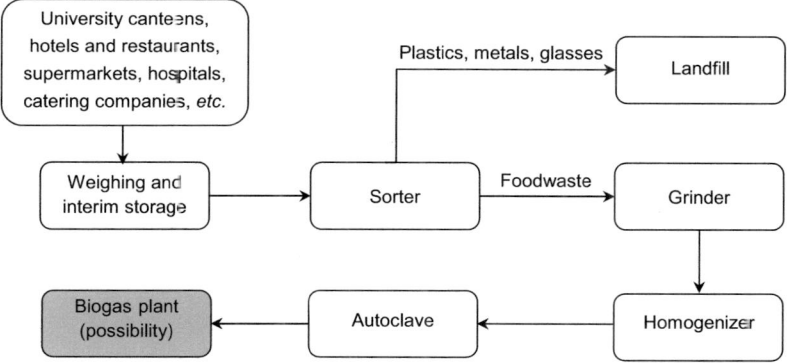

Figure 3.2 Processes overview in a foodwaste collecting company

3.1.3 Press water

One important parameter of OFMSW for a successful composting process is its moisture content since the microbial decomposition of organic matter mainly occurs in the thin liquid films around the surface of the particles (Krogmann and Körner, 2000). To support growth and activity of microorganisms involved in the composting process, OFMSW should have a moisture content within the range of 40 to 60 %. A moisture content below 40 % will severely inhibit the microbial activity, whereas a moisture content above 60 % leads to anaerobiosis and causes leachate and emission of bad odour. Previous research (e.g. Rodriguez-Iglesias *et al.*, 2000, Hansen *et al.*, 2003,

Nordberg and Edström, 2005, Bolzonella *et al.*, 2005) reported that raw OFMSW has a relatively high moisture content of 68 to 75 %, which is too high for a composting process. For compost production the OFMSW must either be mixed with structured support material (which must be sieved off after composting) or dewatered by pressing off surplus water to reach 55 % or less moisture content. If a pressing method is applied, a by-product of pressing leachate will be produced. The pressing leachate will later be called press water. Press water has a high content of suspended and solubilised organic material that requires preferably anaerobic treatment.

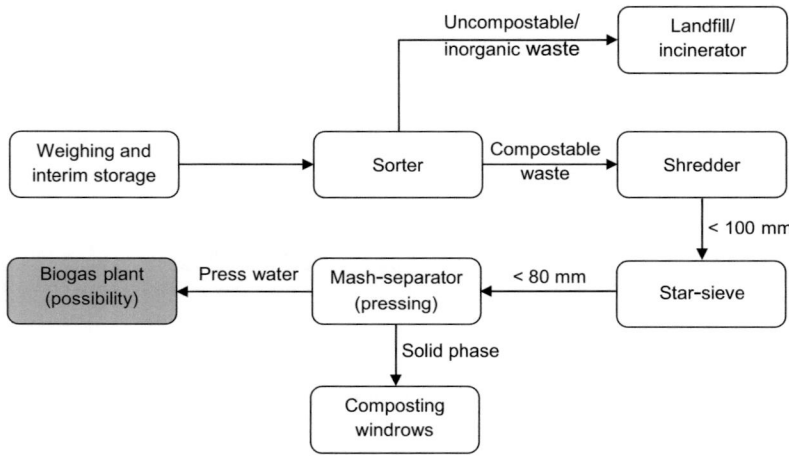

Figure 3.3 Overview of the typical processes involved in the composting plant equipped with mash-separator technique

In this study press water samples were obtained from a composting plant in Grünstadt, Rhineland-Palatinate, Germany. In this composting plant, source-sorted OFMSW from seven municipalities is treated for compost production. A pressing method with mash-separator technique is employed to reduce the moisture content of the delivered OFMSW. A general overview of the processes involved in the composting plant is presented in Figure 3.3. Using this pressing method, from one ton of delivered OFMSW typically 700 kg of solid phase and 300 kg of press water are produced. The daily production of press water in this composting plant is approximately 40 m³.

3.1.4 Potato sludge

The excess sludge from the wastewater treatment plant of a potato processing plant was delivered from a local potato chip company which operated its own wastewater treatment plant. The sludge was taken after the sludge thickening drying bed. A scheme of the wastewater treatment plant is depicted in Figure 3.4.

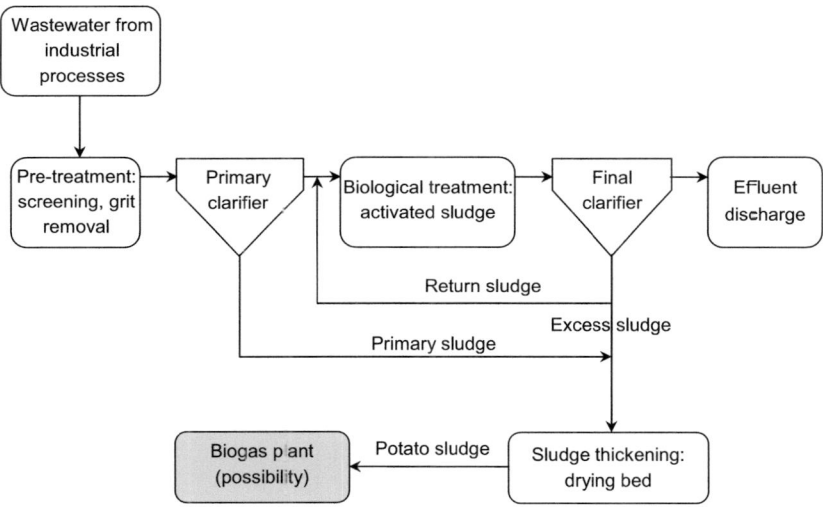

Figure 3.4 Process overview of potato industry wastewater treatment plant

3.1.5 Anaerobic sludge inocula

For batch experiments for biogas (methane) production and the start-up of the reactors, the anaerobic sludge inoculum was obtained from the effluent of a full-scale wet anaerobic digestion plant in Durlach treating source-sorted OFMSW from the city of Karlsruhe, Germany. Before using the digester effluent as inoculum for batch assays and continuous fed-batch reactors, the anaerobic sludge was sieved to remove coarse materials such as leaves, branches, bones, nutshells, *etc*.

For several experiments such as the effect of sludge inoculum storage and the batch experiments of potato sludge effluent from the active laboratory-scale reactors was used as inoculum.

3.2   Laboratory-scale reactors

Two types of laboratory-scale anaerobic reactors were used in this study. These reactors were employed in order to examine the biogas production potential of solid waste substrates, the stability of a substrate as sole substrate in anaerobic digestion, the maximum/optimum organic loading rate and the co-digestion of biowaste with other sources of waste performance.

3.2.1   Schott-glass reactors

The Schott-glass reactors (Mainz, Germany) had a liquid working volume of maximum 3.5 L. The temperature was maintained at 37 °C by thermostated water which was pumped through plastic tubes surrounding the reactor (warm water jacket). The suspension mixing was performed with a magnetic stirrer. Effluent withdrawal and substrate feeding were done by opening the top rubber cover. Biogas produced by the reactor was collected by a gas collector and was leaving the reactor via a gas meter through a water seal which functioned as a barrier to avoid air back flow from the gas meter (see Figure 3.5 A). This type of reactor was employed in the experiment for the biogas production potential of foodwaste and biowaste and also in the experiment of foodwaste stability as the sole substrate in anaerobic digestion.

3.2.2   Glass column reactors

In order to simulate the condition in a full-scale anaerobic digestion reactor, two identical set-ups of laboratory-scale reactors made from vertical glass tubes (inner diameter 0.1 m, total height 1.50 m and 1.70 m, liquid working volume of 8.0 L and 10 L, top and bottom sealed with rubber stoppers) were employed as completely-mixed reactors. The reactors were also equipped with a warm water jacket to maintain the temperature at 37 °C for a mesophilic process.

To obtain a homogeneous suspension, liquid and/or biogas from the top of the reactor was withdrawn by a peristaltic pump and recirculated through the bottom of the reactor. The effluent was withdrawn from an effluent port installed in the recirculation tube by back pumping the suspension. Feeding was done manually after effluent withdrawal from the top of the reactor (Figure 3.5 B). The reactors were also equipped with gas meters and water seals. This type of reactor was employed in the experiments for the biowaste co-digestion with press water and foodwaste (8 L reactor) and the experiment of press water stability as the sole substrate in anaerobic digestion (10 L reactor).

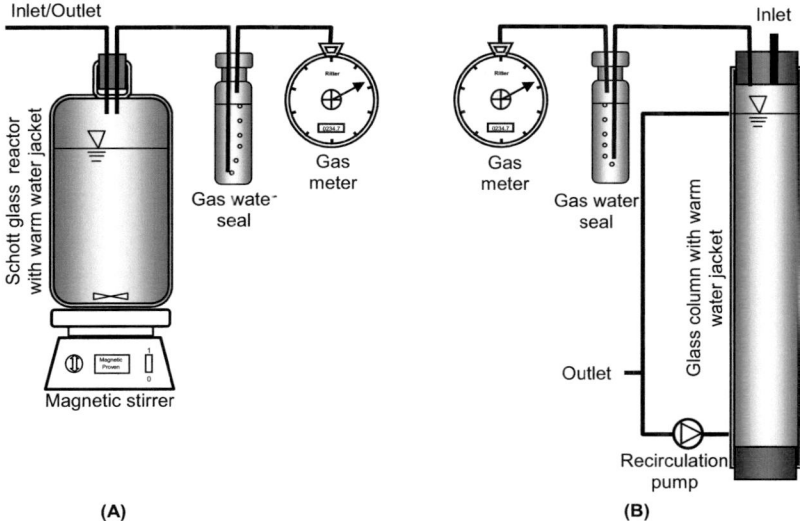

Inlet/Outlet

Inlet

Schott glass reactor with warm water jacket

Gas meter

Gas water seal

Gas meter

Gas water seal

Glass column with warm water jacket

Outlet

Magnetic stirrer

Recirculation pump

(A)

(B)

Figure 3.5 Schematic diagram of reactors used in this study. (A) Schott glass reactor and (B) glass column reactor for simulation of the full-scale reactor operation.

3.3 Experimental designs

3.3.1 Batch assays for the determination of the biogas (methane) production potential of substrates

Biogas productivity from biowaste and foodwaste was examined in batch mode using Schott-glass reactors (3.2 L of total liquid volume). The biogas production potential from biowaste was examined by adding 400 mL of biowaste to 2800 mL of starved inoculum sludge. As for foodwaste, 200 mL foodwaste was added to 3000 mL of inoculum sludge. The cumulative biogas production was observed 2-3 times a day with a wet gas meter and the methane content of the biogas was determined daily using a gas chromatograph. Biogas production was corrected against the same amount of inoculum in a control reactor without fresh substrate addition. Figure 3.6 depicts the set-up of batch assay experiments for biogas production of biowaste and foodwaste. After the biogas production increment of the assays was no longer significant (typically after 2 weeks digestion) the digestate was then mixed as new inoculum to perform similar assays (the batch assay experiment was done three times consecutively).

Figure 3.6 Reactor set-ups for determination of the biogas production potential of biowaste and foodwaste experiment

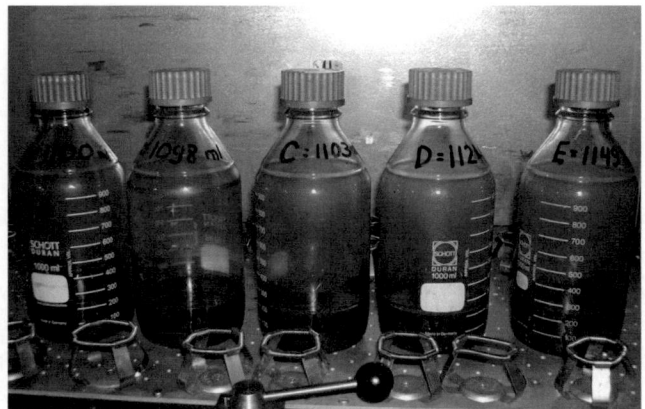

Figure 3.7 Batch assays using Schott bottles for determination of the methane production potential of press water and potato sludge

The potential of methane production of press water and potato sludge was investigated in triplicate assays in Schott-bottles of one liter volume. The test for press water was performed by adding 2.5 mL press water to 247.5 mL of inoculum making the total volume of the assay 250 mL (correspondinf to an additional 0.53 g of chemical oxygen demand, COD or 0.29 g of volatile solids, VS). The test for potato sludge was performed by adding 1.79 g wet potato sludge to an anaerobic sludge inoculum making the total volume of each assay 200 mL (corresponding to an additional 0.48 g cf COD or 0.40 g of VS). In both tests, control assays for methane production frcm the inoculum alone (no addition of substrates) and from the inoculum plus glucose were run. After displacing the head space air with N_2 in order to have anaerobic conditions, the bottles were placed in an orbital shaker and incubated at 37 °C. The cumulative methane production of the essays was measured 2-3 times a day (see sub-chapter 3.4.5 for biogas/methane determination). The set-up of batch assay experiments for determination of the methane production potential of press water and potato sludge is depicted in Figure 3.7.

3.3.2 Stability of foodwaste as a substrate in anaerobic digestion

A Schott glass reactor set-up (3.5 L of total liquid volume) was employed in order tc assess the stability of the biological process (poisoning or inhibition effects during change of the feed from biowaste to food waste), degradability, and specific biogas production of foodwaste during long time continuous feeding. This experiment was performed by feeding the reactor with foodwaste as a sole substrate in a draw-and-fill mode. The reactor was filled with filtered digestate from the full-scale biowaste reactor of the city of Karlsruhe as inoculum. Daily biogas production, methane content, COD, volatile fatty acids and pH were measured in order to evaluate the performance of the reactor. The elimination of solids was examined 2 or 3 times a week.

The reactor was started with biowaste as the sole substrate at an HRT of 8 days After a steady state condition was reached, the feeding of the reactor was continued with appropriately diluted foodwaste (COD values of diluted foodwaste ranged from 84 to 132 g · L^{-1}) in order to maintain the OLR and also to keep the operation of the reactor as wet anaerobic digestion. The biowaste and foodwaste substrates were fed twice a day at 9.00 a.m. and 16.00 p.m. from Monday to Friday (working days of the biowaste digestion plant of Karlsruhe), respectively and feeding was interrupted during weekends as in the full-scale plant.

3.3.3   Co-digestion of biowaste and foodwaste for constant biogas supply

To test the suitability of liquefied foodwaste as a co-substrate in order to fill the biogas production gap during "no-feed" periods (nights and weekends) an 8 L glass column laboratory-scale reactor was employed. According to previous results with the same source of biowaste, the anaerobic digester could be fed with an organic loading rate up to 19 $kg \cdot m^{-3} \cdot d^{-1}$ without any instability (Gallert *et al.*, 2003).

The reactor was started in November 2006 and fed with biowaste at a HRT of 8 days which corresponded to OLR values ranging from 11.7 –13.6 $kg \cdot m^{-3} \cdot d^{-1}$. The variation of OLR values were caused by COD variation of the biowaste suspension from 93.4 $g \cdot L^{-1}$ to 107.1 $g \cdot L^{-1}$. After reaching steady state conditions, co-digestion of foodwaste was tested by feeding the reactor with 1 L of biowaste and 80 mL of foodwaste, resulting an OLR of 16.8 $kg \cdot m^{-3} \cdot d^{-1}$.

During the biowaste-only-fed period, the reactor was fed twice a day at 09.00 a.m and 16.00 p.m., while during the co-digestion period the reactor was fed three times per day: at 09.00 a.m. and 13.00 p.m. with biowaste and at 17.00 p.m. with foodwaste. The co-digestion of foodwaste reduced the hydraulic retention time from 8 to 7.4 days.

3.3.4   Potential use of press water as a substrate in anaerobic digestion

The laboratory fed-batch reactor consisted of a thermostated glass column with a liquid working volume of 10 L. Organic matter degradation (biogas production, COD and VS elimination) at decreasing hydraulic retention time (HRT) and increasing organic loading rate (OLR) was investigated. The glass-column reactor was inoculated with anaerobic sludge from the full-scale digester in Karlsruhe (total VS-amount 125.4 g).

Initially the reactor was fed with 0.5 L of press water (HRT: 20 days) and after the performance of the reactor reached a steady state, the press water feeding was step wisely increased to 1.3 L (HRT: 7.7 days). The feeding of the reactor was done manually twice a day. In the first period (intermittent-feeding period) the reactor was fed 5 days per week and obtained no feeding during weekend, whereas in the second period the reactor was fed twice a day for 7 days per week. Daily measurement of pH, COD and VFA in the effluent and biogas production and as well as biogas composition were analysed before addition of fresh substrate in order to assess the performance of the reactor.

3.3.5 Co-digestion of wet anaerobic digester of biowaste with press water and foodwaste for improvement of biogas production

Almost similar with co-digestion of biowaste and foodwaste for constant biogas supply experiment, a glass column reactor (8 L liquid volume) was employed in order to examine the improvement of biogas production of a wet anaerobic digester treating biowaste if co-digested with press water and foodwaste.

Initially the reactor was fed with only biowaste at HRT of 8 days and after reaching the steady-state, biowaste and press water or foodwaste was added. The biowaste feeding was maintained at 1 L per day (HRT: 8 days) assuming that the full-scale reactor treats relative constant amount of biowaste. Additional substrates such as press water or foodwaste as co-substrates were added to the biowaste suspension before the feeding and mixed well. The increment of co-substrate was done when the performance of the reactor in each increment was considered to be in a steady state condition.

The reactor was fed with the substrate mixture twice a day at 09.00 a.m and 16.00 p.m. Biogas (methane) production, total and soluble COD, pH and VFA of the effluent were measured before addition of fresh substrate.

3.4   Analytical methods

To characterize the wastes and evaluate the performance of the reactors, several parameters were measured and determined, mostly following German Standard Methods for Water, Wastewater and Sludge Analysis (DEV, 1983).

3.4.1 Chemical oxygen demand (COD)

The COD is a measure of the oxidizability of a substrate, expressed as the equivalent amount in oxygen of an oxidizing reagent consumed by a substrate. In this study the COD was determined according to Wolf and Nordmann (1977). Although there is a disturbance potential by the presence of chloride, this method is considered more environmentally friendly since it does not use mercury as a part of the reagent. This method can oxidize organic matter at typically 95-100 % of the theoretical value.

Organic matter was oxidized with potassium dichromate ($K_2Cr_2O_7$) in a mixture of sulphuric acid and phosphoric acid ($H_2SO_4 + H_3PO_4$). Silver sulphate (Ag_2SO_4) was used as a catalyst. After incubating the sample in a thermoblock at 150 °C for 2 hours, the built green Cr^{3+} ions concentration was spectrophotometrically measured at 615 nm (Ultrospec II Spectrophotometer - Biochrom Ltd., Cambridge). The result was then converted to the COD value by comparison with a standard curve of potassium hydrogen phthalate (0 – 1250 mg · L^{-1})

3.4.2 Volatile fatty acids (VFA)

A gas chromatograph (PACKARD model 437A) equipped with a flame ionisation detector (FID) was employed to determine the volatile fatty acid concentration in the sample as described by Gallert and Winter (1997). Mixture of hydrogen (30 mL·$min.^{-1}$) and synthetic air (300 mL·$min.^{-1}$) were used as burning gases. Separation of fatty acids was obtained in a Chromosorb C101 (Sigma, München) Teflon column (2 mm inner diameter x 2 m length). Nitrogen (30 mL·$min.^{-1}$) was used to serve the gas chromatograph as the carrier gas. The temperature was set isothermally at 180 °C for the column and 210 °C for injector and detector.

Sample preparation was as follows: effluent samples were centrifuged. The clear supernatant was acidified 1:1 with 4% H_3PO_4. One μL of acidified sample was injected into the liner in front of the column. The calculation of volatile fatty acids was based on peak area comparison between samples and a mixed volatile fatty acid standard.

3.4.3 Total solids and volatile solids

The solids content of the samples was determined by DEV - Standard Method, DIN 38409 (DEV, 1983). For determining the total solids (TS), samples with certain volume or weight were placed in ceramic vessels and dried in a drying oven (Memmert, Germany) at 105 ± 2 °C for 15 - 20 hours until constant weight. After cooling in the desiccators, the samples were weighed for TS measurement. The samples then oxidized at 550 °C for 2 hours (Heraeus Instruments, Germany) for volatile solids (VS) determination. The volatile solids (VS) were determined by subtraction of the minerals content of the sludge sample (residual ash after oxidation) from the total solids content.

$$ TS = \frac{dv_s - dv_e}{V_s \cdot 1000} \qquad \left[\frac{g}{mL} \right] = \left[g \cdot L^{-1} \right] $$

where,   TS   : total solids
          dv_s : vessel + dried sample weight
          dv_e : empty vessel weight
          V_s : volume of sample

$$VS = \frac{(dv_s - dv_e) - (dv_{s^*} - dv_e)}{V_s \cdot 1000} \qquad \left[\frac{g}{mL} \right] = \left[g \cdot L^{-1} \right]$$

where,

	VS	: volatile solids
	dv_s	: vessel + dried sample weight
	dv_{s^*}	: vessel + ash weight
	dv_e	: empty vessel weight
	V_s	: volume of sample

3.4.4 Biogas production and composition

Biogas production of the reactors was measured daily using a water displacement method by a wet gas meter from Ritter Co. For the experiment of foodwaste co-digestion for constant biogas supply, the gas meter was equipped with a built-in pulse generator and biogas flow rates (daily or hourly flowrates) were measured with a Rigamo V1.15 software .

Biogas composition (methane and carbon dioxide) was analysed with a gas chromatograph (PACKARD model 427) equipped with a Micro-WLD-detector and a Carboplot 007 column (with 0.53 mm of inner diameter and 27.5 m of length) packed with Poropack N (80-100 mesh; Sigma, Deisenhofen). The temperature settings used were as follows: column at 110 °C, injector and detector at 250 °C. Nitrogen served as the carrier gas at a flow rate of 25 mL·min.$^{-1}$.

One hundred μL gas samples were withdrawn from gas sampling ports using a Pressure Lok® syringe (Precsion Sampling Corp., Baton Rouge, Louisiana) and injected into the gas chromatograph. As a reference, a mixture of 60% methane and 40% carbon dioxide was injected under the same conditions to determine the concentration in the samples

3.4.5 Ammonia nitrogen (NH_4-N) and total Kjeldahl nitrogen (TKN)

Ammonia was determined by using a method with preceding distillation. The distillation process was used to separate the ammonia from interfering substances. Ammonia in the sample was distilled into a solution of boric acid and determined titrimetrically with standard H_2SO_4 with a mixed indicator.

Total Kjeldahl Nitrogen (TKN) is used to determine the sum concentration of both organic nitrogen and ammonia nitrogen. The method involves a preliminary digestion to convert the organic nitrogen to ammonia, then distillation of the total ammonia into an acid absorbing solution and determination of the ammonia by titration method. The method employed sulphuric acid as the oxidizing agent. A catalyst was needed to hasten the oxidation of some of the more resistant organic substances. The oxidation proceeded rapidly at temperatures slightly above the boiling point of sulphuric acid (340 °C). The boiling point of the acid was increased by addition of sodium or potassium sulphate. When the organic nitrogen has been released as ammonia nitrogen, it was determined in similar steps to ammonia nitrogen determination as previously mentioned.

3.4.6   pH value

The pH value of the reactor's effluent or of batch experiment was determined electrochemically with an Ingold pH electrode. As the check reference, pH paper was also used to determine the pH value.

3.4.7   Heavy metals concentration

Heavy metals (Cr, Cu, Mn, Fe, Co, Ni, Cd, Pb and Zn) were analysed by flame or graphite-furnace atomic absorption spectrometry using a Varian Spectra AA 220 FS (Mulgrave, Australia). The spectraAA was equipped with an air-acetylene burner with an air flowrate of 13.5 $L \cdot min^{-1}$ and an acetylene flowrate of 2 $L \cdot min^{-1}$. There was a chimney on top of the sample compartment to protect one from heat and UV radiation emitted by the burning process. After performing calibration with standard solutions, the sample solution was atomized in the burner and a light of element-specific wavelength was emitted and quantified.

Preparation of samples in order to measure total heavy metals concentration of sludge sample was done by first cooking the sample for 2 hrs after the addition of 21 mL of 37 % HCl and 7 mL of 65 % of HNO_3 (nitrohydrochloric acid; Ger.: *Königswasser*). Circulated water tubes were placed as cover of the beakers to condense back the vapour leaving the samples. After the samples cooled to room temperature, the samples were filtered with 210 mm diameter folded filters (pore diameter. 0.45 μm), then Millipore water (Milli-Q, Germany) was added to the required dilution. For the measurement of soluble heavy metal concentrations, samples were centrifuged two or three times to get a clear supernatant and diluted to a concentration that could be detected by the Spectra AA. Further dilutions were done when concentrations were above the detection limits.

3.4.8 Acid capacity (Ger.: *Säurekapazität* - $KS_{4,3}$)

$KS_{4,3}$ is a method to measure the overall buffering capacity against acidification of a solution (in this study: effluent from the bioreactors). The acid capacity was analyzed according to DIN 38409-7 (DEV, 1983). The effluent of the reactor (200 mL) was titrated with hydrochloric acid (HCl 0.5 M) until the pH value reached 4.3.

The $KS_{4,3}$ of the biowaste reactor's effluent was determined by the following formula:

$$KS_{4,3} = \frac{V_t \cdot C_{HCl}}{V_s} \cdot 1000 \qquad \left[\frac{mL \cdot (mol \cdot L^{-1})}{mL} \right] = \left[mmol \cdot L^{-1} \right]$$

where, V_t : volume of hydrochloric acid titration

C_{HCl} : concentration of hydrochloric acid

V_s : volume of effluent sample

3.5 Basic parameter calculations

3.5.1 Hydraulic retention time (HRT)

HRT is the average residence time of the waste suspension in the bioreactor. It is calculated by comparing the liquid volume of the reactor and the effluent withdrawal.

$$HRT = \frac{V_r}{Q_w} \qquad \left[\frac{m^3}{m^3 \cdot d^{-1}} \right] = \left[day(s) \right]$$

where, HRT : hydraulic retention time

V_r : liquid volume of the reactor

Q_w : effluent withdrawal

3.5.2 Organic loading rate (OLR)

OLR is the amount of organic matter (COD or VS), that is loaded to one volumetric unit of reactor per time unit. The OLR is calculated using the following formula:

$$OLR = \frac{OC_{fd} \times Q_{fd}}{V_r} \qquad \left[\frac{kg \cdot m^{-3} \times m^3 \cdot d^{-1}}{m^3} \right] = \left[kg \cdot m^{-3} \cdot d^{-1} \right]$$

where,   OLR   : organic loading rate
           OC_{fd} : COD or VS concentration of the substrate
           V_r : liquid volume of the reactor
           Q_{fd} : substrate feeding rate

3.5.3 Organic matter removal efficiency

As one of reactors' performance measures COD and/or solids removal efficiency of the reactors was calculated using the following formula:

$$\eta = \frac{OC_{in} - OC_{ef}}{OC_{in}} \times 100\% \qquad \left[\% \right]$$

where, OC_{in} : organic matter (COD, VS) concentration of feed substrate
           OC_{ef} : organic matter (COD, VS) concentration of reactor's effluent

Chapter 4

RESULTS AND DISCUSSION

4.1   Potential use of foodwaste as a co-substrate for constant biogas supply

As has been discussed previously (see sub chapter 1.4), a scheme of "waste-to-energy" concept has been applied in the city of Karlsruhe. This concept comprises the use of landfill gas and biogas from the biowaste digestion plant as well as the use of heat from wood waste incineration for electricity and steam supply. However, the biogas supply from the sanitary landfill will continuously decrease and cease in 10-20 years. In addition, a problem of inconstant biogas supply from the biowaste treatment plant has to be anticipated also if the present collection mode is not changed. The biogas production in semi-continuously-fed anaerobic digestion plants varies during work days due to the feeding mode resulted from work hours (*e.g.* from 7.00 a.m. to 21.00 p.m.), during a week due to a deficiency of biowaste suspension at weekends and throughout the year, due to seasonal variation of organic matter in biowaste.

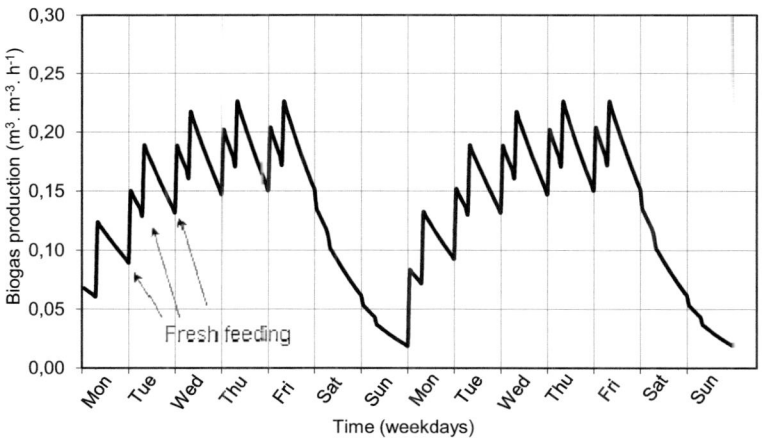

Figure 4.1 Typical biogas production rates in a semi-continuously-fed anaerobic digestion plant

Figure 4.1 illustrates the variation of biogas production rates of a semi-continuously fed anaerobic digester. In this illustration, it is assumed that the digester is fed twice a day (e.g. 9.00 a.m. and 16.00 p.m.). After the introduction of fresh feeding, the biogas production increases to reach a peak production in a certain time. After the peak is reached, the biogas production decreases gradually. In the early morning or from Saturday to Monday morning biogas production is very little (even near zero) because of a deficiency of digestible fresh biowaste supply. At a semi-continuous feeding regime during regular work hours and insufficient storage capacities for biowaste suspensions very little biogas is available during weekends and neither electricity nor heat can be supplied. The little produced biogas cannot be optimally operated as well.

In order to produce more biogas and/or filling the gap of decreasing biogas production during night times and on weekends for a more efficient and optimal operation of power and heat generators, a semi-continuously-fed biogas reactor might be fed during these times with easily and automatically handlable biodigestible co-substrates. In this study, foodwaste was selected as co-substrate with the assumption that it has relatively high concentration of organic substances with a good biodegradability. Foodwaste can be obtained with enough quantity, can be stored intermittently and have a high methane production potential. With these assumptions, it was expected that feeding the biogas plant with foodwaste as co-substrate will equalized and improve the biogas production without any negative effect.

4.1.1   Characteristics of foodwaste and biowaste suspension

Table 4.1 presents the main characteristics of the two substrates (i.e. biowaste and foodwaste) used in this study. Concerning the total and soluble COD, the foodwaste was about three-fold more concentrated than the different batches of biowaste. On average, the total nitrogen content of food waste was also about threefold higher, so that after dilution to the COD of biowaste the similar COD:N-ratio was resulting. In biowaste, varying amounts of propionate were present, whereas in foodwaste almost no propionate was found.

Due to the collection method and its mechanical pre-treatment of biowaste in a hydropulper, the proportion of soluble or very fine particulate COD of biowaste suspension tended to be a little higher than that in food waste (40 % versus 35 %, respectively). In the city of Karlsruhe, source-sorted OFMSW (organic fraction of municipal solid waste) from households is collected every 14 days. This collection interval enables the hydrolysis process to occur prior to mechanical pre-treatment in the anaerobic digestion plant. During pre-treatment of biowaste in a hydropulper part of the particulate organic matter was disrupted or hydrolysed to soluble or colloidal compounds that could not or not rapidly be sedimented by centrifugation.

Table 4.1 Main characteristics of biowaste and foodwaste

Characteristic	Unit	Biowaste[1]	Foodwaste[2]
COD $_{total}$	$g \cdot L^{-1}$	77-111	350
COD $_{soluble}$	$g \cdot L^{-1}$	30-45.5	120
Total solids	$g \cdot L^{-1}$	50-90	255
Volatile solids	$g \cdot L^{-1}$	40-70	225
NH_4^+-Nitrogen	$g \cdot L^{-1}$	0.32	0.22
Total Kjedahl nitrogen	$g \cdot L^{-1}$	2.3	7.8
Fat	$g \cdot g^{-1}$ TS	0.031 – 0.047	0.2 – 0.25
pH	-	4.2	5.6
Acetic acid	$g \cdot L^{-1}$	1.80 - 4.11	2.60
Propionic acid	$g \cdot L^{-1}$	0.22 – 1.59	0.05
Butyric acid	$g \cdot L^{-1}$	0 – 0.35	0
Valeric acid	$g \cdot L^{-1}$	0- 0.08	0.05

[1] After hydropulping, the low and high values of different analyses correspond with each other, respectively

[2] After thermal hygienization.

As has been discussed in the previous sub-chapter, this study was aimed to simulate the full-scale anaerobic digester in Karlsruhe-Durlach. This full-scale digester applied a wet anaerobic digestion system. According to Vandevivere *et al.* (2002) a wet anaerobic digestion system should be fed with organic slurries containing less than 15 % total solids to maintain a gradient-free suspension. Thus, i) to facilitate hydropulping of biowaste and ii) to operate a completely mixed methane reactor, one portion of fresh biowaste was suspended with 2 portions of process water for hydropulping and methane fermentation. The TS values of the biowaste slurries after hydropulping ranged from 5 - 9 %.

Foodwaste contained 25.5 % total solids, and if it is fed undiluted as the sole substrate to an anaerobic digester, it would be suitable for a dry digestion system (Vandevivere et al., 2002). Since foodwaste consisted mainly of left-over food and undigested food residues, it is evident that foodwaste had a much higher fat content than biowaste suspension (Table 4.1).

From an economic point of view, daily supply of foodwaste as co-substrate for anaerobic digestion is not feasible due to high transportation costs. Therefore, storage of foodwaste as co-substrate has to be considered. During the storage time of the co-substrate, biological processes may occur. It will be more beneficial for an anaerobic digester plant if the co-substrate does not lose its organic materials during storage, thus the digester will not loose its biogas production potential.

Table 4.2 presents the stability of foodwaste during storage in closed Schott-bottles at room temperature. The test was done in two different methods of storage: foodwaste only and a mixture of foodwaste and biowaste. Biogas production and the pH value of each storage mode were measured daily. Initial and final concentrations of volatile fatty acids were also measured. The pH value of foodwaste dropped from initially 5.60 to 4.10 after 2 weeks of storage. The same trend occurred also in the mixture of foodwaste and biowaste (the pH dropped from 4.90 to 4.00). The decrease of pH is most probably due to the acidification process especially acetogenesis, which occurred in both storage methods. The acetic acid concentration during storage of foodwaste only increased from 2.60 $g \cdot L^{-1}$ to 3.19 $g \cdot L^{-1}$ while during storage of the mixture it increased from 3.63 $g \cdot L^{-1}$ to 5.78 $g \cdot L^{-1}$. The increase acetic acid concentration during storage of the mixture mode was presumably caused by the conversion of propionic acid, butyric acid and valeric acid to acetic acid.

The decrease of the pH was actually an advantage for the storage of foodwaste since it preserved the organic material content from being released as methane. This low pH value allowed very little activity of methanogenic bacteria. There was only a maximum of 0.31 % of methane development observed during storage of foodwaste while in the foodwaste and biowaste mixture there was no methane development observed. The low value of pH apparently was responsible for the releases of CO_2 as the main biogas product from foodwaste and biowaste.

Table 4.2 pH and VFA variation of foodwaste and biowaste during a storage-stability test

Day to:	Foodwaste							Foodwaste + Biowaste *						
	pH	Biogas (%)		Volatile fatty acids (g · L^{-1})				pH	Biogas (%)		Volatile fatty acids (g · L^{-1})			
		CH$_4$	CO$_2$	HAc	HPr	HBr	HVl		CH$_4$	CO$_2$	HAc	HPr	HBr	HVl
1	5.60	-	-	2.60	0.05	0.00	0.05	4.90	-	-	3.63	1.03	0.22	1.29
3	5.01	0.18	10.5					4.50	-	12.7				
4	4.62	0.31	23.8					4.31	-	24.3				
5	4.51	-	40.5					4.20	-	42.6				
7	4.39	-	48.2					4.14	-	45.4				
13	4.19	-	54.4	3.19	0.09	0.00	0.87	4.00	-	55.9	5.78	0.83	0.12	0.23

* : the mixture was 1:1 (v/v)

HAc : acetic acid
HPr : propionic acid
HBr : butyric acid
HVl : valeric acid

4.1.2   Biogas production potential of biowaste and foodwaste

The biogas production potential of biodegradable solid wastes depends on the content
of digestible carbohydrates, lipids and proteins, as well as on the content of more
resistant cellulose, hemicellulose and lignin (Gallert and Winter, 1999; Hartmann and
Ahring, 2006). Figure 4.2 depicts the biogas production with time from the biowaste
suspension of the biowaste treatment plant of Karlsruhe in a batch assay experiment.
The figure shows that after 2-3 days, already more than 90 % of the biogas was
released. In the following 2-3 days the biogas production ceased and even upon
prolonged incubation no biogas was evolved any more.

This biogas productivity was in accordance with that of the full-scale biogas plant of
Karlsruhe during weekends, when no substrate was added (Gallert *et al.*, 2003, Gallert
and Winter 2008). The maximum biogas production potential was 0.39 $m^3 \cdot kg^{-1}$ COD or
0.59 $m^3 \cdot kg^{-1}$ VS_{added}. The highest biogas production rate was obtained within the first
48 hours with 0.35 $m^3 \cdot kg^{-1}$ $COD \cdot d^{-1}$. The average methane content of the biogas
produced by digestion of biowaste during the batch experiment was 62 %.

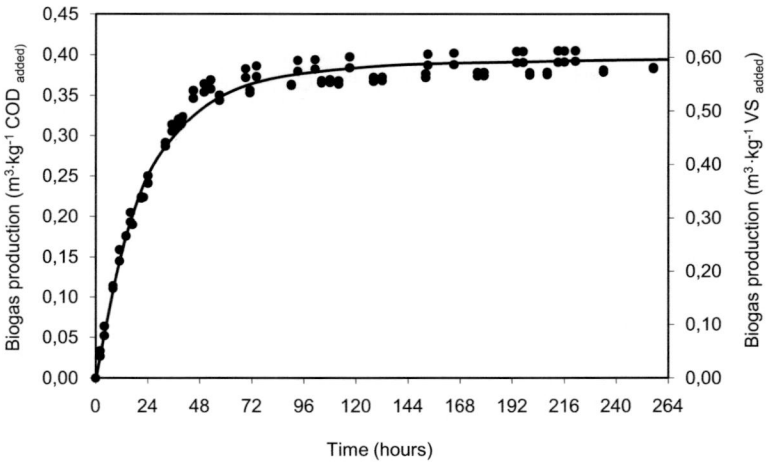

Figure 4.2 Biogas production potential of biowaste

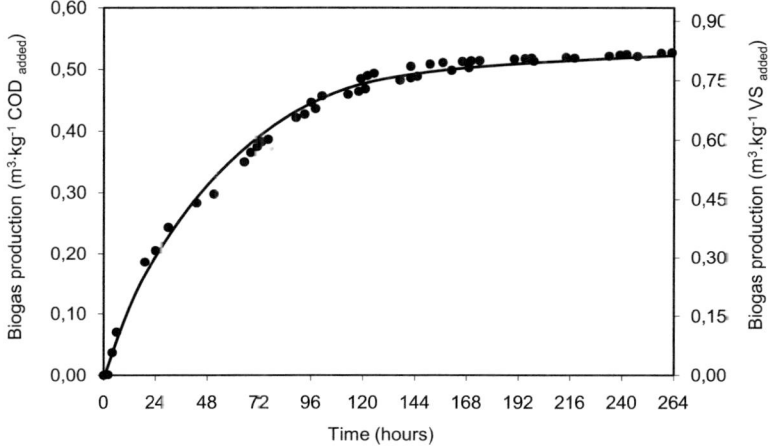

Figure 4.3 Biogas production potential of foodwaste

Compared to the biogas production of biowaste, foodwaste produced little less biogas during the first 48 hours of digestion (0.29 $m^3 \cdot kg^{-1}$ COD_{added} versus to 0.35 $m^3 \cdot kg^{-1}$ COD_{added}). With feeding of only foodwaste, about 50 % of the biodegradable compounds were digested within 48 h (Figure 4.3) and biogas production continued at decreasing rates for about 5 days, before it levelled off to almost zero. After 10 days of digestion, foodwaste cumulatively yielded more biogas than biowaste (0.51 $m^3 \cdot kg^{-1}$ COD_{added} versus 0.39 $m^3 \cdot kg^{-1}$ COD_{added}). The average methane content of the biogas from food waste was 66 %, and thus was also a little bit higher than that of biowaste. This was caused by, at an identical pH, higher fat content of the foodwaste since the biogas production from carbohydrates or protein theoretically cannot not exceed 0.746 $m^3 \cdot kg^{-1}$, while triglycerides as the main constituent of vegetable oil and animal fats, can reach up to 1.434 $m^3 \cdot kg^{-1}$ (Gallert and Winter, 2000)

The degradability of foodwaste was approximately 20 – 30 % higher than that of biowaste. This might have been due to the higher concentration of digestible fat in foodwaste. To achieve the higher biogas amount or conversion efficiency of organics with foodwaste a relatively long digestion time of around 6 days was required; as compared to about 3 days with biowaste (compare Figure 4.2 and Figure 4.3).

4.1.3   Stability of foodwaste as a substrate in anaerobic digestion

To test the stability of the degradation process in the biowaste digester during change of the feed from biowaste to food waste, a Schott-bottle reactor (with a total liquid working volume of 3.5 L) was fed for the first two weeks with biowaste as the sole substrate at 8 days of HRT. After a steady state was reached, the feeding of the reactor was then continued with appropriately diluted foodwaste to maintain the same organic loading and HRT. After a dilution with tap water, the COD values of diluted foodwaste ranged from 84 to 132 g · L⁻¹. The biowaste and foodwaste substrates both were fed twice a day at 9.00 a.m. and 16.00 p.m. from Monday to Friday (working days of the biowaste digestion plant of Karlsruhe), respectively and feeding was interrupted during weekends as in the full-scale plant.

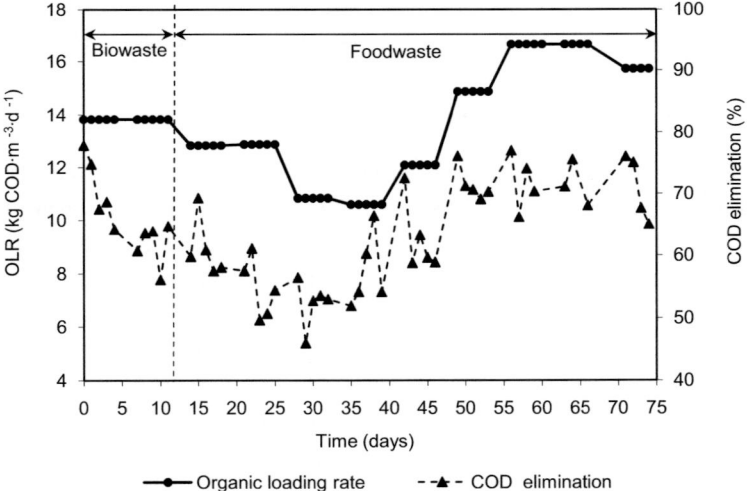

Figure 4.4 COD elimination in BR1 after feed change from biowaste to food waste at changing organic loading rates. The hydaulic retention time was kept constant at 8 days by respective dilutions of the foodwaste.

Figure 4.4 presents the changes of OLR and related COD elimination during the experiment. The biowaste suspension for start-up had a COD of 110 g · L⁻¹, which corresponded to an initial OLR of 13.8 kg · m⁻³ · d⁻¹. A steady state was obtained after one week with about 62 % COD-removal. Two weeks after the start-up, the biowaste substrate was changed to diluted foodwaste (1:3.5) with a COD of 102 g · L⁻¹, corresponding to an OLR of ⁻2.9 kg · m⁻³ · d⁻¹.

COD elimination during foodwaste feeding varied over a broad range. Within the first 15 - 20 days of foodwaste feeding, the COD removal efficiency decreased from over 60 % to around 50 %. The OLR was then maintained at around 10.7 kg · m⁻³ · d⁻¹ by adjusting dilution of foodwaste to reach a COD value of 85 g· L⁻¹. After an improving COD removal for several days the OLR was stepwise increased. Finally, for an OLR of 16 kg · m⁻³ · d⁻¹ (Figure 4.4, from 55 days onwards) the COD elimination reached an average of 70 %.

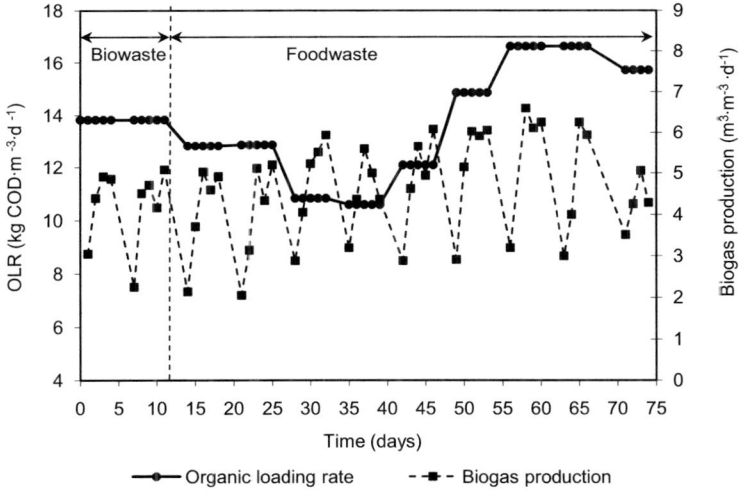

Figure 4.5 OLR and volumetric biogas production of BR1

Figure 4.5 presents the variations of biogas production related to OLR. Similar as in the full-scale biowaste digester in Karlsruhe-Durlach, the daily biogas production fluctuated due to a deficiency of fresh substrate during the no-feeding period at weekends. The average biogas production reached approximately 4.6 m³ · m⁻³ · d⁻¹ when the reactor was fed at an OLR of 10.7 kg · m⁻³ · d⁻¹. The daily biogas production increased to 4 8 pH and VFA variation of foodwaste and biowaste during a storage-stability test and 5.2 m³·m⁻³· d⁻¹, respectively when the OLR was increased to 12.2 and 14.9 kg · m⁻³ · d⁻¹. The fluctuation of daily biogas amounts was not higher at high OLR compared to lower OLR.

Figure 4.6 presents volatile fatty acid concentrations for the different loading rates of biowaste and food waste during the experiment. During the start-up, no butyric and valeric acid was detectable. The initially present acetic acid was rapidly degraded, whereas the propionate concentration increased to 1,793 mg · L^{-1}. When propionate degradation began after 5 days, acetic acid was accumulating instead, presumably from propionate decarboxylation. Acetic acid reached a maximum concentration of 1.153 mg · L^{-1}. As has been reported by several authors (*e.g.* Inanc *et al.* 1999 and Gallert *et al.*, 2003), the accumulation of fatty acids is normally occurring during start-up periods or process instability following shock loading. The methanogenic population was reported to be inhibited at propionic acid concentrations in excess of 1.000 mg · L^{-1}. Although there was accumulation of acetic and propionic acid during start-up and every successive OLR increment (propionic acid reached 1,793 mg · L^{-1} during start-up and 1,037 mg · L^{-1} after OLR increment to 16.6 kg · m^{-3} · d^{-1}), the reactor did not show any shock loading symptoms and the performance of the reactor (COD elimination and biogas production) was not drastically deteriorated.

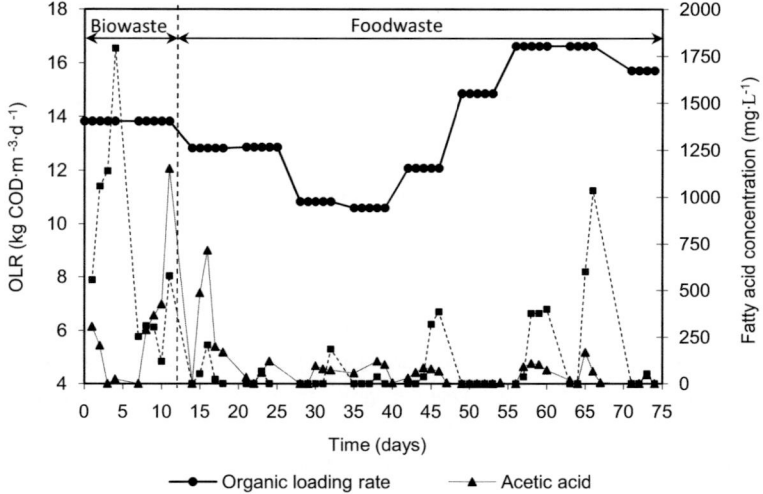

Figure 4.6 Organic loading rate and concentration of volatile fatty acids of BR1

4.1.4 Co-digestion of biowaste and food waste: Loading regime and biogas production

Loading regime of the reactor. The glass column laboratory-scale reactor (with a total liquid working volume of 8.0 L) was started with biowaste as the sole substrate. After reaching steady state conditions, co-digestion of biowaste and foodwaste was started. During the steady-state condition, the reactor was fed with biowaste at an HRT of 8 days corresponded to OLRs of 11.7 –13.6 $kg \cdot m^{-3} \cdot d^{-1}$, caused by COD variation of the biowaste suspension from 93.4 $g \cdot L^{-1}$ to 107.1 $g \cdot L^{-1}$. According to previous results with the same source of biowaste, the reactor could be fed with an OLR up to 18 $kg \cdot m^{-3} \cdot d^{-}$ without any instability (Gallert *et al.*, 2003). For co-digestion of biowaste with foodwaste, the reactor was fed with 1 L of biowaste (corresponding to a HRT of 8 days) and 80 mL of foodwaste, resulting in an organic loading rate of 16.8 $kg \cdot m^{-3} \cdot d^{-1}$. During the biowaste-only-fed period, the reactor was fed twice a day at 09.00 a.m and 16.00 p.m., while during the co-digestion period the reactor was fed three times per day: at 09.00 a.m. and 13.00 p.m. with biowaste and at 17.00 p.m. with foodwaste. The co-digestion of foodwaste reduced the HRT from 8 days to 7.4 days (Figure 4.7).

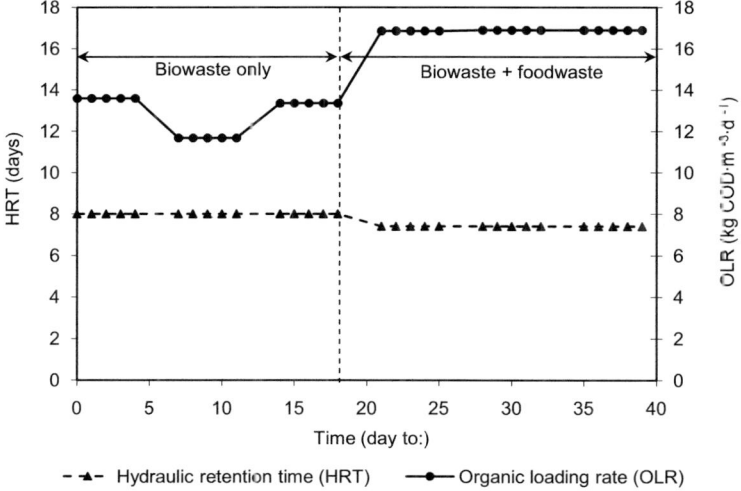

Figure 4.7 Loading regime of BR2 during co-digestion experiment

Biogas production. In Figure 4.8 hourly biogas production rates of the reactor during 3 weeks of biowaste feeding, followed by three weeks of biowaste + foodwaste feeding were projected upon each other. The hourly biogas production of foodwaste varied from 0.027 $m^3 \cdot m^{-3} \cdot h^{-1}$ to 0.456 $m^3 \cdot m^{-3} \cdot h^{-1}$. Minimal gas production rates were observed on each Monday morning, when the reactor has been starving since Friday night. After resuming the biowaste feeding, maximal gas production rates were reached one hour after the 2nd daily feeding at around 16.00 p.m. and then the biogas production rate decreased slowly until the next morning. Since the last feeding during every working day was at 16.00 p.m., the biogas production decreased to a minimum rate of approximately 0.105 $m^3 \cdot m^{-3} \cdot h^{-1}$ until the next morning, before feeding was continued at 9.00 a.m.

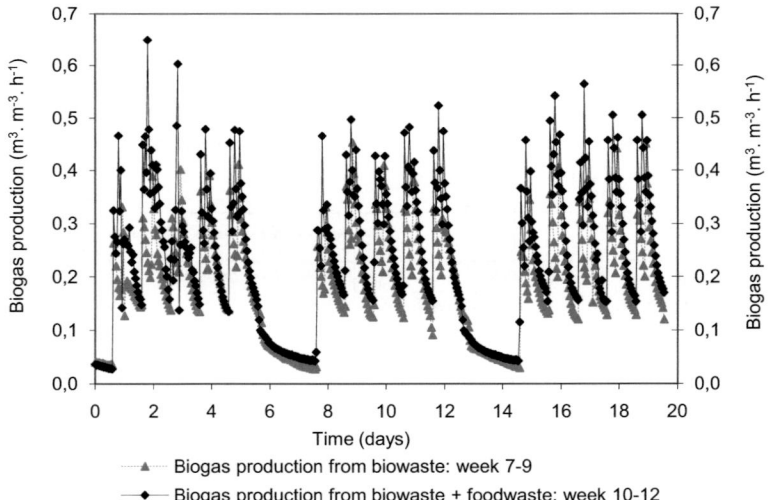

- ▲ Biogas production from biowaste: week 7-9
- ◆ Biogas production from biowaste + foodwaste: week 10-12

Figure 4.8 Comparison of hourly biogas production between the biowaste-only-fed period and co-digestion of biowaste and foodwaste

The hourly biogas production rates were slightly higher when foodwaste as co-substrate was fed into the reactor. The minimum biogas production rate after the weekend was 0.042 $m^3 \cdot m^{-3} \cdot h^{-1}$, whereas the minimum daily gas production rate after 10 h starvation was 0.135 $m^3 \cdot m^{-3} \cdot h^{-1}$. The highest gas production rates were between 0.55 and 0.65 $m^3 \cdot m^{-3} \cdot h^{-1}$. The highest biogas production rate at all was measured on the third day of co-fermentation of foodwaste. The shape of the biogas production curves of the reactor fed with biowaste or during co-digestion of foodwaste was similar.

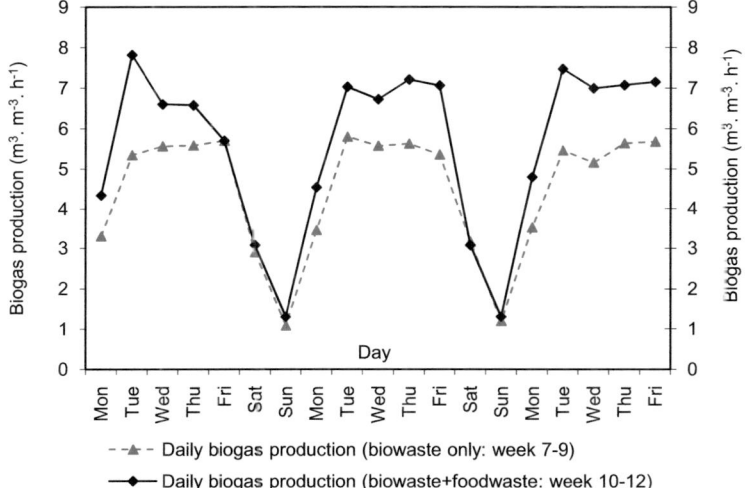

Figure 4.9 Comparison of daily biogas production in the reactor fed biowaste only (triangles) and in the reactor fed biowaste + foodwaste (squares)

Figure 4.9 shows daily biogas rates during biowaste-only-fed periods and co-digestion periods, projected upon each other. From the graph it can be concluded, that, although the hourly biogas production during the co-digestion period only slightly increased, on a daily basis the biogas production increased significantly. During a biowaste-only-fed period, the daily biogas production reached its minimum value of 1.09 $m^3 \cdot m^{-3} \cdot d^{-1}$ on Sundays and the maximum values during the week (5.62 - 5.70 $m^3 \cdot m^{-3} \cdot d^{-1}$). During the first week of foodwaste addition, the daily biogas production increased immediately to 7.82 $m^3 \cdot m^{-3} \cdot d^{-1}$ but came down to the level of biowaste-only-feeding at the weekend (Figure 4.9). The decrease of gas production was accompanied by less COD elimination and higher fatty acid concentrations in the effluent due to the necessity of the population to adapt to the new substrate and to cope with the higher organic loading rate (Figure 4.10 and 4.11, day 20 onwards). In the second and third week of foodwaste co-digestion the performance of the reactor had stabilized and the daily biogas production of the reactor increased by 21 - 37 % compared to the level of biogas production during biowaste-only-fed periods.

4.1.5 Co-digestion: COD and volatile solids elimination

The success of solid waste digestion is mainly dependent on the removal of soluble organics and of suspended solids. If the solids in the effluent of a treatment plant have to be deposited in a landfill, high solid reduction will be beneficial in terms of handling, transportation and volume requirement in a sanitary landfill. Elimination of biodegradable organic matter is also important in order to fullfil the requirement of the European Landfill Directive.

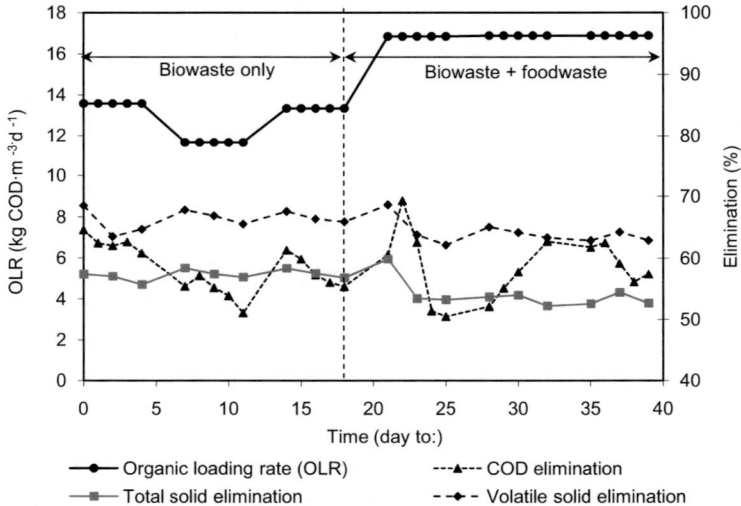

Figure 4.10 COD and volatile solid elimination of the biowaste reactor before and during co-digestion of foodwaste

The COD elimination efficiency of the reactor ranged from 51% - 65% (average 56%) during the biowaste-only-fed periods. Typically COD elimination decreased throughout weekdays and within a week (Figure 4.10). This phenomenon happened due to incomplete degradation of the substrate from the previous day(s). After the start of foodwaste addition, the COD elimination efficiency of the reactor decreased to its lowest value of 50 %. However, in the 2nd week of co-digestion, the elimination efficiency increased throughout weekdays from 52 to 62 %. This indicated that the reactor was able to cope with the additional OLR from foodwaste (should be compared also with biogas production and fatty acid concentration in the effluent: Figure 4.9 and

Figure 4.11). During the 3rd week of co-digestion, the COD elimination efficiency of the reactor reached the same level as in biowaste-only-fed periods.

Volatile solid elimination during biowaste-only-fed periods was 63 % - 68 % with a typical decrease of elimination similar to COD elimination). In line with its volatile solid elimination efficiency, the reactor had a total solid elimination efficiency ranging from 56 % - 58 %. During co-digestion of foodwaste, the volatile solid elimination efficiency of the reactor slightly decreased to a range of 62 % - 65 % with a total solid elimination efficiency of 52 % - 54 %. Considering the high OLR during the co-digestion, this slight decrease of solid elimination efficiency can be regarded as insignificant.

4.1.6 Co-digestion: Volatile fatty acids

During biowaste-only-fed operation of the reactor, the dominant volatile fatty acids in the effluent were acetic and propionic acid. The concentrations of acetic and propionic acid reached their maximum values of 198 mg $\cdot$ L^{-1} and 422 mg $\cdot$ L^{-1} at the end of each day or week and disappeared completely during the weekend, when no substrates were added. The increasing concentrations for acetate and propionate during the week can still be considered as low, indicating that the acetogenic and methanogenic population in the reactor was intact. Other volatile fatty acids such as i- and n-butyric and valeric acid were not present in the reactor effluent.

When the reactor was fed a mixture of biowaste and foodwaste, in the first week of foodwaste co-digestion the concentration of acetic and propionic acid increased to 715 mg$\cdot$L^{-1} and 2,660 mg$\cdot$L^{-1}, respectively (Figure 4.11). The increase of fatty acid concentrations was caused by the higher organic loading rate and the new type of substrate, which apparently differed from biowaste. However, after 3 days the concentration of acetic acid decreased to nearly the same level as the previous concentration without foodwaste addition. Propionic acid removal required about 1 week time to reach the low steady-state concentration levels and was completed about 2 weeks after foodwaste introduction.

As shown in Figure 4.11, the pH was almost constant throughout the experimental period, ranging from 7.3 to 7.5. Only during the first week of co-digestion, the pH decreased to 7.1 and came back again to 7.3 – 7.5 in the following week. The decrease of the pH value during the first week of co-digestion was caused by residual volatile fatty acids in the effluent, especially by high concentrations of propionic acid.

According to Dinamarca *et al.* (2003) and the experience from this study, it is not necessary to control the pH throughout steady-state operation, since the pH is kept stable by the buffer effect of biowaste and foodwaste.

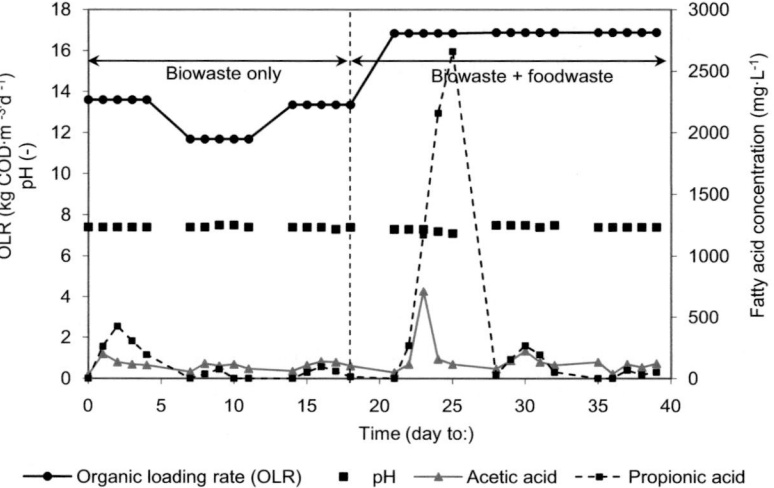

Figure 4.11 Volatile fatty acid concentrations and pH development of the reactor before and during co-digestion of foodwaste with biowaste

4.1.7 Anaerobic treatment of foodwaste for energy recovery: experiences from previous studies

Foodwaste, including uneaten food and food preparation leftovers from residences, commercial establishments such as restaurants, institutional sources like school cafeterias, and industrial sources like factory lunchrooms, is considered as the largest component of the waste stream by weight (Zhang *et al.*, 2007). In the United States for example, more than 43.6 million tons of foodwaste was produced each year (US EPA, 2002), while the United Kingdom generates more than 5.3 million tons of foodwaste per year (Hogg *et al.*, 2007). Wang *et al.* (1997) reported that according to several authors, the concentration of foodwaste increased to between 40 and 85% of the total solid waste generated in developing countries. Since foodwaste is an organic-rich solid waste which has a relatively high energy content, it seems ideal to achieve dual benefits from energy recovery and waste stabilization. Due to the relative high moisture content of foodwaste, anaerobic digestion is a more suitable treatment compared to thermo-chemical treatment technologies, such as combustion and gasification.

Anaerobic digestion as a method to recover energy from foodwaste has been widely examined and reported in many papers. Some of the papers focused on the characteristics and methane production potential of foodwaste as a substrate in anaerobic digestion (e.g. Cho et al., 1995 and Zhang et al., 2007). The physical and chemical characteristics of foodwaste are important information for designing and operating anaerobic digesters, because they affect biogas production and process stability. Some authors reported the effects of operational parameters such as temperature, pH and HRT on the anaerobic digestion of foodwaste process (e.g. Zhang et al., 2005 and Kim et al., 2006). Other authors reported some technologies and methods to improve the performance of anaerobic digestion of foodwaste, including leachate recirculation, co-digestion and modification of process stages (e.g. Wang et al., 2002; Kim et al., 2003; Dearman and Bentham, 2006 and Kim et al., 2008).

Table 4.3 presents remarkable results from some selected publications reporting anaerobic digestion of foodwaste for the recovery of methane. Compared to the results presented in the table, the methane yields in this study (both, from batch assays and the semi-continuous reactor) were within the range. From the table, it can be seen that potential methane yields of various foodwaste sources ranged from 0.21 – 0.54 $m^3 \cdot kg^{-1}$ VS_{added}. In this study, the maximum methane production potential from batch tests was 0.54 $m^3 \cdot kg^{-1}$ VS_{added}, while methane yields during semi-continuous operation of 3.5 L reactor ranged from 0.27 – 0.50 $m^3 \cdot kg^{-1}$ VS_{added} with an average of 0.36 $m^3 \cdot kg^{-1}$ VS_{added}.

Table 4.3 Selected reports on anaerobic digestion of foodwaste for methane recovery

Source of foodwaste	Type of process	Remarkable results	Author(s)
Dining hall	· Laboratory batch tests · Fed with various mixtures of food waste and sewage sludge at concentration of 1.4 g VS· L⁻¹ and 2.0 VS· L⁻¹ · Mesophilic (35 °C) and thermophilic (55 °C)	· Predicted optimal mixture of foodwaste and sewage sludge: fractions of food waste at 2 g VS · L⁻¹ were 39.3% in mesophilic and 50.1% in thermophilic conditions, respectively · Max. CH₄ yield: 0.26 m³· kg⁻¹ VS_added (mesophilic with 80 % foodwaste), 0.34 m³· kg⁻¹ VS_added (thermophilic with 80 % foodwaste)	Kim *et al.*, 2003
Foodwaste management company	· Laboratory batch tests · VS loading: 6.8 and 10.5 g· L⁻¹ · Thermophilic (50 ± 2 °C)	· The average C/N ratio of foodwaste ca. 14.8 · Average VS reduction: 86 % · Max. CH₄ yield: 0.35 and 0.44 m³· kg⁻¹ VS_added after 10 and 28 days of digestion, respectively.	Zhang *et al.*, 2007
Synthetic restaurant waste with different component excesses	· Laboratory batch tests · VS loading: 1.35 g VS/g VS inoculum · Mesophilic (37 °C)	· Foodwaste with excess of lipids showed slower methane production and higher COD in the liquid. · Hydrolysis rate constants: 0.12 d⁻¹ (excess of lipids), 0.18 d⁻¹ (excess of cellulose), 0.22 d⁻¹ (excess of proteins) and 0.32 d⁻¹ (excess of carbohydrates) · VS reduction: 94.0- 99.6 % · Max. CH₄ yield: between 0.40 m³· kg⁻¹ VS_added (excess of carbohydrates) and 0.49 m³· kg⁻¹ VS_added (excess of lipids)	Neves *et al.*, 2007
Meat and bone meal (MBM) from foodwaste management company	· Laboratory batch tests · Organic loading: 1%, 2%, 5% and 10% of MBM solid content · Mesophilic (35 °C)	· Reversible CH₄ inhibition was observed at higher solid loading (*i.e.* 5 % and 10%), presumably due to an inhibition caused by the increase of VFA and NH₃ concentrations · VS reduction: 79.0 -9 2.0 % · CH₄ yield: 0.35 - 0.38 m³· kg⁻¹ VS_added	Wu *et al.*, 2009
University and hospital kitchens	· Modification of SEBAC (sequencing batch anaerobic composting) · Mesophilic (37 °C)	· Increasing leachate exchange rate between mature and start-up reactors will shortened the time to reach methanogenesis · CH₄ yield: 0.21-0.23 m³· kg⁻¹ VS_added	Dearman and Bentham, 2007

Table 4.3 Selected reports on anaerobic digestion of foodwaste for methane recovery (cont.)

Source of foodwaste	Type of process	Remarkable results	Author(s)
University canteen	- Hybrid two-phase anaerobic batch reactor system (leachate recycle reactor and UASB) - HRT: 6-8 days - Mesophilic (35 °C)	- Removal efficiencies: 77–79% of TOC, 57–60% of VS and 79–80% of COD. - 99% of the biogas generated was from the methanogenic phase with 68–70% CH_4 content. - CH_4 yield: 0.25 $m^3 \cdot kg^{-1}$ VS_{added}	Wang et al., 2002
Typical Korean food as foodwaste representation	- Hybrid two-phase anaerobic digestion system (solid-bed reactor and upflow blanket filter) - OLR: 1.04 – 3.39 kg VS $\cdot m^{-3} \cdot d^{-1}$ - Mesophilic (37 °C)	- In the leach-bed two-phase anaerobic digestion, the degradation rate depended on the recycle flow rate and the HRT of methane reactor - VS reduction: 89.2–90.0 % - CH_4 yield: 0.36-0.37 $m^3 \cdot kg^{-1}$ VS_{added}	Cho et al., 1995
University restaurant	- Two-phase semi-continuous feeding reactor - Controlled pH at: 5, 7, 9, 11 - OLR: 16.5 kg VS $\cdot m^{-3} \cdot d^{-1}$ - Mesophilic (35-37 °C)	- With controlled-pH at 7, relatively high hydrolysis and acidogenesis rates were obtained - VS reduction: 88.6 % - Max. CH_4 yield: 0.54 $m^3 \cdot kg^{-1}$ VS_{added}	Zhang et al., 2005
University canteen	- Modified two-phase anaerobic digester named hybrid anaerobic solid–liquid (HASL) system - Mesophilic (35 °C)	- Enhancement of hydrolytic and fermentation processes in the acidogenic reactor when food waste was frozen for 24 h at -20 °C and then thawed for 12 h at 25 °C in comparison with fresh food waste - Frozen/thawed pre-treatment of food waste gave an opportunity to shorten operational time of batch process by 42%	Stabnikova et al., 2008
Typical Korean foodwaste	- Modified three-stage methane fermentation system: semi-anaerobic hydrolysis, anaerobic acidogenesis and strictly anaerobic methanogenesis - HRT: 8 -12 days - Mesophilic to thermophilic (30-55 °C)	- Thermophilic digesters had a higher rate of organic material removal efficiency than mesophilic digesters - Methane production rates of thermophilic digesters were higher than those by mesophilic digesters regardless of HRT - VS reduction: 76.0 – 78.0 % - Max. CH_4 yield: 0.40 $m^3 \cdot kg^{-1}$ VS_{added} (at 50 °C and 12 d of HRT, calculated using COD/VS ratio and VS reduction)	Kim et al., 2006

4.2   Anaerobic digestion of press water from a composting plant

Large-scale municipal solid waste composting has been recognized a useful alternative to the disposal of organic solid wastes in to sanitary landfills. Through composting, several advantages in solid waste management such as the recycle of organic matters, the destruction of pathogen as well as volume and mass reduction can be achieved. Therefore, especially for the members of the European Union, composting is very attractive since it could have a vital role in meeting the obligations of the EU Landfill Directive.

The history of large-scale municipal solid waste composting in Europe was originated in the Netherlands in the end of 1920s. This composting facility was used to treat municipal solid wastes from several cities and to produce compost for which a great demand for land reclamation projects existed. The attempts to make the best use of composting technologies to treat unsorted municipal solid waste in Europe began in the 1970s and extended into the 1980s. The method to process the entire municipal solid waste streams, including unsorted solid waste, is now known as mechanical and biological treatment (MBT) process. The main element of the MBT process involves mechanical separation of the organic matter fraction from the municipal solid waste for composting or anaerobic digestion process. The MBT plants also undertake limited recycling of some materials from the MSW such as ferrous metals and plastics and some would produce a refuse derived fuel (RDF) from the remaining light fraction (Slater and Frederickson, 2001).

In Europe, Germany is categorized as an advanced composting country since it has installed a wide range of composting plants from simple windrow systems to highly sophisticated technical processes. Several technologies and methodologies have been applied in order to optimize the composting process and to improve the quality of compost. Gruneklee (1997) reported that in 1995 already around 28 % of the municipal composting plants in Germany were categorized as technically advanced. In 2006 a total number of 485 OFMSW treatment plants (both anaerobic digesters and composting plants) participated in the State Commission for Delivery Terms and Quality Assurance (Ger.: RAL-*Reichsausschuß für Lieferbedingungen und Güte-sicherung,*) for compost, fermentation products and humus (Ger.: *RAL-Gütesicherungen für Kompost, Gärprodukte und AS-Humus*). These plants treated altogether 7.8 million tons of biodegradable waste. The majority of this amount (approx.

5.9 million tons) generated predominantly from source-sorted OFMSW as well as garden and park wastes and was treated in composting plants (BGK, 2007).

Although composting has been considered as an established technology, the application of composting for municipal solid waste has not always been fully successful. The principal causes of the unexpected result include: low quality of inputs (e.g. the present of foreign matters such as glass splinters or plastic fragments, the high moisture content and the elevated concentration of heavy metals), inappropriate application of the technology which could produce low quality or even harmful products and low revenues from the sale of compost to offset operating costs (Mato et al., 1994; Renkow and Rubin, 1998; Krogmann, 1999).

One technical effort to improve the composting process is by reducing the moisture content of raw OFMSW materials, which is normally above 60 %, in order to avoid anaerobiosis, which lead to the emission of bad odour and caused low quality of the compost product. This effort can be achieved either by mixing the raw OFMSW with structured support material (which must be sieved off after composting) or dewatering method by pressing off surplus water to reach 55 % or less moisture content. If a pressing method is applied, a by-product of pressing leachate (later be called press water) will be produced. A detailed explanation of the processes involved in a composting plant equipped with pressing facility is presented in sub-chapter 3.1.2.

Since press water has a high content of suspended and solubilised organic material, anaerobic treatment is preferred over aerobic treatment due to its energy recovery potential in the form of methane, less area requirement and less emission of bad odor and green house gasses. This sub-chapter presents the main characteristics of the press water, its biogas productivity and an assessment of the suitability of press water as a substrate of anaerobic digestion for the recovery of its energy potential and to reduce handling problems.

4.2.1   Characteristics of press water

The parameters of the composition of press water are presented in Table 4.4. Approximately half of the total COD was soluble, as was found earlier for another source of OFMSW (Gallert and Winter, 1997). This may indicate that hydrolysis must have started already during collection, weighing and interim storage and may have preceded with high hydrolysis rates after the pressing procedure due to the small particle size in the suspension, obtained by the applied mash-separator technique. Palmowski and Müller (2000) reported that size reduction of materials with high fibre content will improve degradability up to 50 % and biogas productivity by 20 %. The authors also assumed that size reduction did not only release biodegradable cell compounds in a more easy and rapid way but also supported hydrolysis of suspended solid compounds in the long term. In line with the high soluble COD content of press water there was an accelerated acidification process, indicating by the presence of relatively high concentrations of total VFA (9.51 $g \cdot L^{-1}$) with acetic acid as the predominant organic acid (8.56 $g \cdot L^{-1}$).

Table 4.4 Main characteristics of press water

Parameter		Unit	Value
pH		-	4.3
Density		$ton \cdot m^{-3}$	1.02
Chemical oxygen demand		$g \cdot L^{-1}$	213.4
Soluble COD		$g \cdot L^{-1}$	100.1
Total solids		$g \cdot L^{-1}$	168.4
Volatile solids		$g \cdot L^{-1}$	117.7
Ashes		$g \cdot L^{-1}$	50.7
Total Kjeldahl nitrogen		$g \cdot L^{-1}$	4.10
$TKN_{soluble}$		$g \cdot L^{-1}$	1.52
Ammonia nitrogen		$g \cdot L^{-1}$	0.72
Acetic acid		$g \cdot L^{-1}$	8.56
Propionic acid		$g \cdot L^{-1}$	0.16
Butyric acid		$g \cdot L^{-1}$	0.21
Valeric acid		$g \cdot L^{-1}$	0.58
	wet volume	$mL \cdot L^{-1}$	3.0
Sand sediment	dry weight	$g \cdot L^{-1}$	4.40
	volatile fraction	$g \cdot L^{-1}$	0.05

The sand content of press water was analyzed using a gentle washing method since, due to the consistency and the grayish dark color of the press water, sedimentation test in Imhoff cones did not lead to a clearly visible layering. The sand content is an important parameter since the sand might sediment in the less turbulent zones of biogas digesters. This reduces the working volume and the nominal HRT of the reactor causing degradation of the digester performance. Even if fluidization could be maintained properly, sand would cause abrasion of pipe bends or moving mechanical equipment such as pump impellers, which consequently would increase maintenance costs and time loss due to reparation.

Table 4.5 Heavy metals concentration in press water - comparison of inhibitory and toxicity concentrations for anaerobic digestion

Parameters	Press water (mg·L^{-1})		Inhibitory (mg·L^{-1})[a]	Toxic (mg·L^{-1})[a]
	Total	Soluble		
Iron	1249	291.0	n.a.	n.a.
Zinc	59.6	42.0	150-400	250-600
Nickel	96.4	13.4	10-300	30-1,000
Cobalt	22.2	12.8	n.a	n.a
Copper	29.4	15.2	40-250	170-300
Cadmium	1.9	1.3	-	20-600
Lead	15.0	15.0	300-340	340
Chromium	13.1	9.8	100-300	200-500
Manganese	202.6	134.0	n.a.	n.a.

[a] after Kouzeli-Katsiri and Kartsonas (1986)

Table 4.5 presents some important heavy metal concentrations in the press water. Many heavy metals are essential for anaerobic digestion since heavy metals affect the activity of enzymes which are required for proper energy metabolism of organisms that drive anaerobic reaction sequences (Oleszkiewicz and Sharma, 1990). Takashima and Speece (1989) investigated heavy metals in cells of ten methanogenic strains. They showed the presence of the following heavy metals (in falling concentration): Fe >> Zn ≥ Ni > Co = Mo > Cu. A proper dosage of heavy metals is required for anaerobic processes. Nickel ions at a concentration of 5 mg·L^{-1} for instance will stimulate methane production by *Methanobacterium thermoautotrophicum* to its optimum production (Oleszkiewicz and Sharma, 1990).

Although the presence of heavy metals in organic matter may cause stimulation for anaerobic digestion, it was also observed that heavy metals in higher concentration may cause inhibition or even exert toxic effects. Aquino and Stuckey (2007) collected data from several publications and concluded that the action of heavy metals as nutrients or toxicants was affected by many factors, such as the total metal concentration, the environmental conditions (pH and redox potential), the kinetics of precipitation, complexation and adsorption. Moreover, Kouzeli-Katsiri *et al.* (1988) noted that the toxicity of a heavy metal for anaerobic digestion depends upon several important factors such as the chemical form in which the metal exists in sludge or in the digester, the acclimation ability of organisms and the possibility of antagonism and synergism among heavy metals. Stronach *et al.* (1986) considered already that only the soluble part of metals was bio-available and thus relevant for anaerobic bacteria in the digester.

From Table 4.5, it can be seen that almost all of the essential metals (except for molybdenum, which was not measured) were available in the press water. With the exception of iron and nickel, the heavy metal concentrations (both, total and soluble) were relatively low and far from inhibitory or toxic amounts.

4.2.2   Potential methane production of press water

The results of methane production from press water in batch experiments are presented in Figure 4.12. The maximum methane yield was achieved during the first two days of the digestion (ca. 0.18 m^3-CH$_4$ · kg^{-1} VS$_{added}$·d^{-1}). About 90% of the maximum methane production was released in the first four days. After seven days digestion there was no longer a significant methane production observed and it was decided that after two weeks of digestion, the potential methane production of press water already reached its maximum.

The maximum net potential methane production of press water was approximately 0.27 m^3 CH$_4$·kg^{-1} COD$_{added}$ and this corresponded to 0.49 m^3 CH$_4$· kg^{-1} VS$_{added}$. Compared to the methane production potential of biowaste and foodwaste, the value from press water lies in between (biowaste has maximum methane production potential of 0.37 m^3

$CH_4 \cdot kg^{-1}$ VS_{added} while foodwaste revealed a maximum methane production of 0.52 m^3 $CH_4 \cdot kg^{-1}$ VS_{added}). This indicated that lipids were also present in the press water since the methane production value exceeding the theoretical value from carbohydrates and proteins (see also sub-chapter 4.1.2).

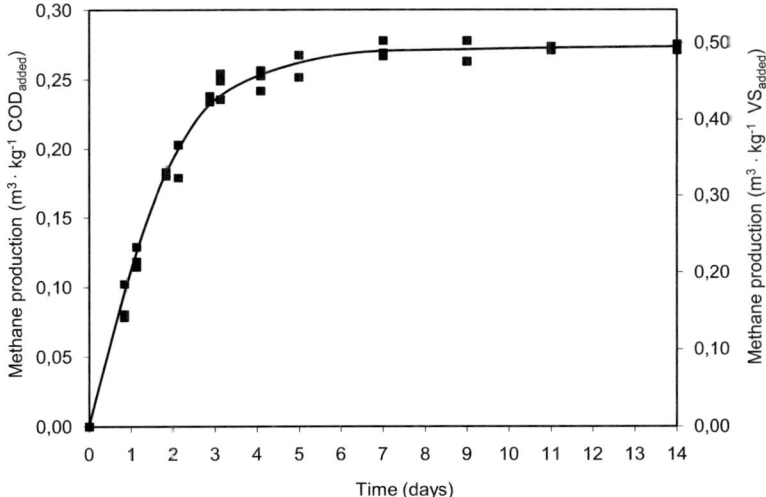

Figure 4.12 Methane production potential of press water. Curves represent methane production from press water only and were obtained by subtracting methane production in assays with and without press water addition.

Using similar batch experiments to determine the maximum methane production of source-sorted OFMSW, Hansen *et al.* (2003) reported that the results ranging from 0.299 to 0.544 m^3 -$CH_4 \cdot kg^{-1}$ VS_{added} depended on the pre-treatment method applied to the raw solid waste (disc screen, screw press device and magnetic separation with shredder). The average value appeared to be around 0.45 m^3 $CH_4 \cdot kg^{-1}$ VS_{added}. The methane potential test, however, was conducted at much longer time than the tests for press water (over 50 days compared to 14 days). The authors also determined the chemical composition of the OFMSW and it was reported that for most of the samples the measured methane production reached 75–90% of the theoretical methane potential (calculated using Buswell's formula).

4.2.3   Loading regime of the laboratory-scale reactor

Figure 4.13 presents the variation of HRT and OLR during the experiment with the laboratory-scale reactor. The reactor was operated for about five months with semi-continuous feeding. Initially the reactor was fed with an OLR of 10.7 kg COD · m^{-3} · d^{-1}, then it was increased step-wise to a final OLR of 27.7 kg COD · m^{-3} · d^{-1} (from 5.9 kg VS · m^{-3} · d^{-1} to finally 15.3 kg VS · m^{-3} · d^{-1}). Each increment was performed when the reactor has been considered in steady-state conditions. The steady-state condition was derived from the COD elimination efficiency, relatively stable biogas production, methane content of the biogas, pH of the digestate and concentration of residual VFA in the effluent. The increment of the OLR required an increasing press water feeding from 0.5 L · d^{-1} to 1.3 L · d^{-1}, which corresponded to a reduction of the HRT from 20 to 7.7 days. Until day 97, the feeding of press water was only during working days (from Monday to Friday) as a simulation of the full-scale plant, which operates only at working days. From day 98 onwards at an of OLR 21.3 kg COD · m^{-3} · d^{-1} and higher the reactor was fed 7 days per week (also fed at weekends).

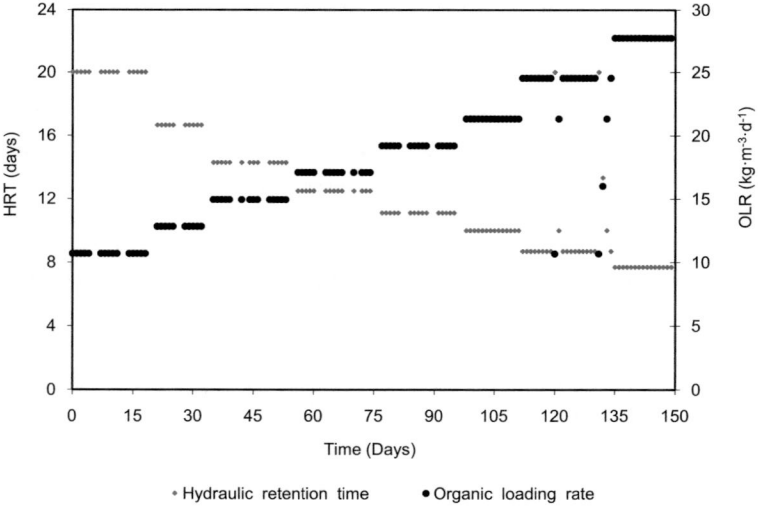

• Hydraulic retention time   • Organic loading rate

Figure 4.13 Loading regime during the semi-continuous feeding experiment

4.2.4   Performance of the laboratory-scale reactor: biogas production

Biogas and methane production at increasing OLRs to more than 25 kg COD $\cdot$ m^{-3} $\cdot$ d^{-1} during the semi-continuous feeding experiment are shown in Figure 4.14. The average biogas yield and its methane content for each HRT are listed in Table 4.6.

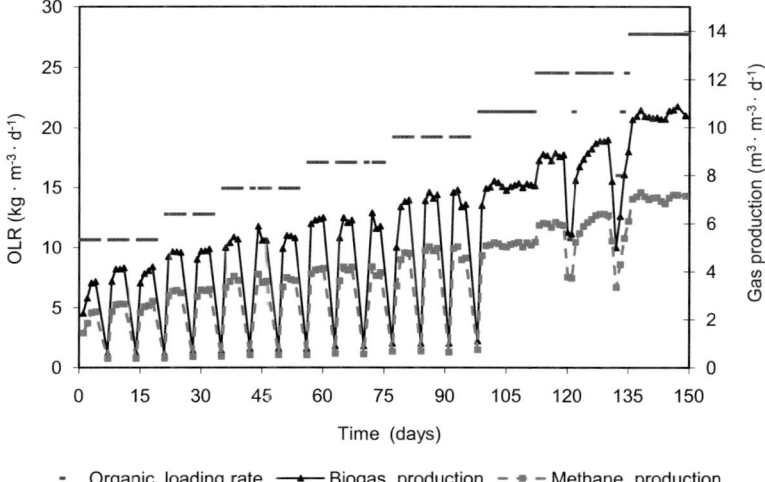

Figure 4.14 Variations of daily volumetric biogas and methane production at increasing OLR.

From Figure 4.14, it is evident that the volumetric biogas production rate of the reactor increased linearly with the increment of the OLR. The average volumetric biogas/methane production rate increased from 4.08 m^3 biogas $\cdot$m^{-3}$\cdot$d^{-1} (2.64 m^3 CH$_4$ $\cdot$ m^{-3}$\cdot$d^{-1}) at the lowest OLR (10.7 kg COD $\cdot$m^{-3}$\cdot$d^{-1}) to 10.44 m^3 biogas $\cdot$ m^{-3} $\cdot$ d^{-1} (7.24 m^3 CH$_4$ $\cdot$m^{-3}$\cdot$d^{-1}) at the highest OLR (22.7 kg COD $\cdot$m^{-3}$\cdot$d^{-1}). Although the OLRs were different, the specific biogas and methane yield was relatively stable at values between 0.647 m^3 -biogas $\cdot$ kg^{-1} VS and 0.696 m^3 biogas $\cdot$ kg^{-1} VS (0.438 m^3 CH$_4$ $\cdot$ kg^{-1} VS and 0.450 m^3 CH$_4$ $\cdot$ kg^{-1} VS).

Compared to the methane production potential of press water, the values of the methane yield from the semi-continuous reactor reached 89.6 % to 91.8 % of the maximum methane production value (0.49 m^3-CH$_4$ $\cdot$ ton^{-1} VS$_{added}$). This indicated that the initially inoculated population contained sufficient amounts of all organisms that were required for efficient press water biodegradation or that a rapid population shift occurred in the reactor when fed-batch-feeding of press water was started.

On day 119 and day 130 there were aeration accidents in the reactor. After clogging of the gas outlet tube by a massive production of foam, the upper rubber stopper was lifted off. The air was pumped by recirculation-pump from the top of the open reactor through the press water reactor content for 6 to 10 hours. After the reactor was repaired, the OLR was reduced to 10.7 kg COD $\cdot m^{-3} \cdot d^{-1}$ and then was increased back to 24.4 kg COD $\cdot m^{-3} \cdot d^{-1}$ in large increments. After only 3-4 days of the feeding increments, the biogas production and methane composition reached their high value from before the disturbance.

Table 4.6 Average biogas yield and methane content at each HRT

HRT (days)	OLR [COD] $(kg \cdot m^{-3} \cdot d^{-1})$	OLR [VS] $(kg \cdot m^{-3} \cdot d^{-1})$	Biogas production $(m^3 \cdot m^{-3} PW^a \cdot d^{-1})$	Biogas yield $(m^3 \cdot kg^{-1} VS)$	CH_4 (%)
20.0	10.7	5.9	81.5	0.696	64.6
16.7	12.8	7.1	80.8	0.691	65.8
14.3	14.9	8.2	76.8	0.656	67.4
12.5	17.1	9.4	76.7	0.656	65.8
11.1	19.2	10.6	77.8	0.665	66.8
10.0	21.3	11.8	75.7	0.647	67.7
8.7	24.5	13.5	76.3	0.652	67.9
7.7	27.7	15.3	80.3	0.686	67.6

[a] PW = press water

4.2.5   Performance of the laboratory-scale reactor: residual volatile fatty acids

Figure 4.15 presents the residual volatile fatty acids concentrations in the effluent of the press water bioreactor. Although the analysis was done for four different volatile fatty acids (acetate, propionate, butyrate and valeriate), only acetate and propionate were detected in significant amounts. In the first week, propionate concentration increased to more than 2,500 mg·L^{-1}. However, this relatively high propionate concentration seemed not to inhibit the biogas production or to influence the overall anaerobic process. Within a few days the propionate decreased to a non-measurable concentration, indicating that the propionate-degraders within the group of acetogenic bacteria had adapted their activity to the new situation (*i e.* the change of substrate from biowaste to press water). Butyrate and valeriate were not measurable at any time. These acids were either not produced as intermediate products or their acetogenic conversion to acetate and hydrogen proceeds were much faster at any time than their generation (Gallert and Winter, 2005).

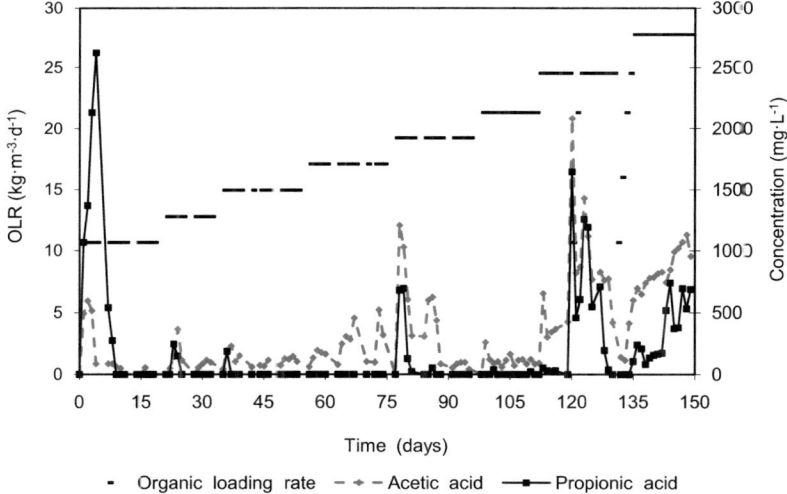

Figure 4.15 OLR and residual volatile fatty acids in the effluent.

As expected, the concentration of propionate and/or acetate increased suddenly at each stepwise increase of the OLR (Figure 4.15). This indicated that the capacity of the propionate and acetate degrading bacteria of the consortium apparently was exceeded for a short while, but a fast recovery within a few days was possible. These two bottle neck reactions may have been caused by limited activities the syntrophic propionate degraders and by the aceticlastic methanogens. However, most of the time during steady-state conditions, the propionate concentration was at unmeasurable level.

Another sudden increase of both acetate and propionate concentrations occured when oxygen came accidentially into the reactor (*i.e.* on day 119 and 130). Since the oxigenation on day 119 was longer, the VFA sudden increase was also more notable. The concentration of acetate increased to more than 2,000 mg · L^{-1} and of propionate to more than 1,500 mg · L^{-1}. However, by reducing the OLR for 2 days, the concentration of acetate and propionate decreased to their normal low level within less than two weeks. Biogas and methane production decreased immediately after the oxygenation, but recovered fast (see also Figure 4.14).

4.2.6 Performance of the laboratory-scale reactor: Removal efficiency of organic compounds

The removal efficiency of organic compounds was measured daily by determining the elimination of total COD. When steady-state conditions at each HRT were reached, based on stable values for pH, residual fatty acids, biogas production and COD elimination, total solids and volatile solids of the reactor effluents were also determined. Figure 4.16 presents the daily COD elimination efficiency at different OLR levels.

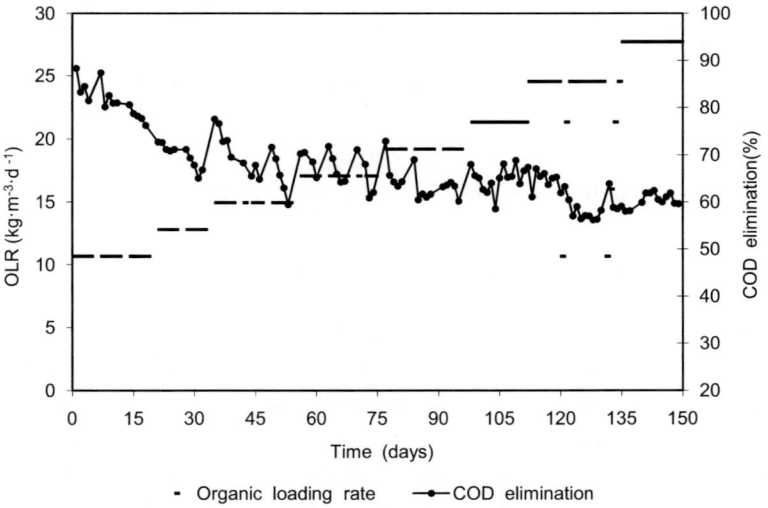

Figure 4.16 OLR and COD elimination efficiency.

In the first weeks of the operation, the reactor apparently reached a relatively high COD elimination of more than 75 %. The high COD elimination in the start-up period was probably due to the high inoculum-substrate ratio and the dilution of the feeding substrate with the inocula which had a lower COD value. At all level of OLRs, during the time of intermittent feeding from Monday to Friday, the COD elimination varied from 60 % to 70 %. The highest COD elimination was measured on every Monday since there was no fresh feeding in the weekend. When the feeding was supplied semi-continuously for seven days a week, the COD elimination reached a stable value of around 60 % to 65 %.

Presented in Figure 4.17 is the relationship between solids elimination (TS and VS elimination) and different OLR values. Assuming that a VS elimination of 50 % to 60 % is considered as close to the optimum for anaerobic degradation of press water, it can be concluded that the OLR of the reactor should be within the range of 13.5 to 22.5 kg COD $\cdot$ m^{-3} $\cdot$ d^{-1} (7.5 to 12.4 kg VS $\cdot$ m^{-3} $\cdot$ d^{-1}). This relatively high OLR value for optimal organic matter removal supports the conclusion of Hartmann and Ahring (2006) that high-solids anaerobic processes appear to be more efficient when a reactor is operated at an OLR higher than 6 kg VS $\cdot$ m^{-3} $\cdot$ d^{-1}.

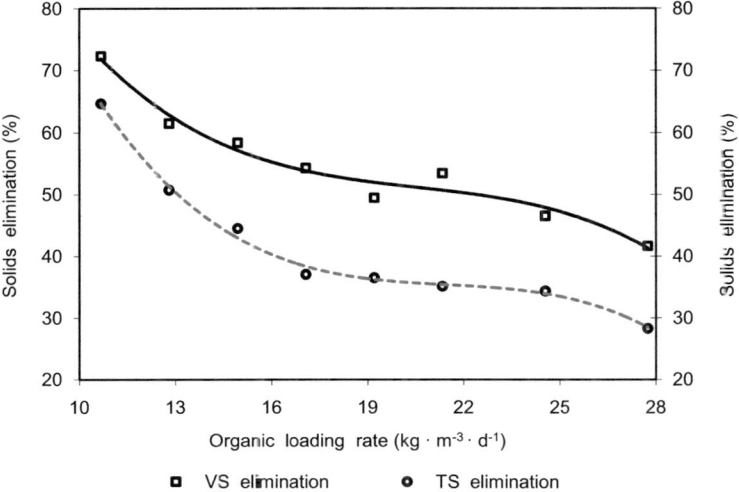

Figure 4.17 Total solids and volatile solids elimination at increasing OLR.

4.2.7   Comparison with other wet anaerobic digestion of solid waste

According to Vandevivere *et al.* (2002), a reactor is categorized as a wet anaerobic digester if treating solid waste with a TS less than 15 %. Although the raw press water had a TS value of 17 %, immediately after batch wise feeding to the reactor twice a day the reactor content had a maximum solid content of 11 %. Therefore, semi-continuous anaerobic digestion of press water can be considered as a wet system.

Table 4.7 presents some selected reports on wet anaerobic digestion of various solid wastes. Solids removal, methane yield and methane production rate are also presented in the table as the most important parameters in judging the successful operation of an anaerobic digestion reactor of high-solids wastes. The HRTs from these studies vary from 4.5 to 30 days and the OLRs vary from 1.31 to 12.6 kg VS $\cdot$ m^{-3} $\cdot$ d^{-1}. However, most of the studies applied HRTs of more than 10 days with much lower OLRs compared to the anaerobic digestion of press water in this study. Although the methane yield values and VS elimination of these studies were not far from those of press water, the methane production rates had distinct difference. Most of the studies had methane production rate even lower than 2.0 m^3 CH$_4$ $\cdot$m$^{-3}\cdot$d^{-1} while anaerobic digestion of press water had the lowest value of 2.64 m^3 CH$_4$ $\cdot$ m$^{-3}\cdot$d^{-1} and reached a maximum methane production rate of 7.24 m^3 CH$_4$ $\cdot$m$^{-3}\cdot$d^{-1}.

The low methane production rates from the studies in Table 4.7 were caused by low OLR values resulting from low degradation rate of the substrates. In anaerobic digesters which treat substrates with low degradation rate, it is difficult to reach high OLR since the application of high OLR potentially deteriorate the performance of the digester. A study on anaerobic digestion of fruit and vegetable waste by Mtz.-Virtutia *et al.* (1995), for example, reported that although the digesters perform well at an OLR of 3.1 kg VS $\cdot$ m^{-3} $\cdot$ d^{-1} (HRT 17.9 days) the performance of the digesters in terms of methane yield started to worsen when the OLR was increased to 6.3 kg VS $\cdot$m$^{-3}\cdot$d^{-1}. The digester showed a symptom of failure (as indicated by very low methane yield and VS elimination) when the OLR was increased to 12.6 kg VS $\cdot$m$^{-3}\cdot$d^{-1}. This comparison allows a conclusion that press-water is a suitable substrate for anaerobic digestion due to its high degradation rate and its possibility to be applied at high OLR. Most probably, the high degradation rate of press water is caused by its small particle size, in line with the report from Palmowski and Müller (2000) that size reduction of materials with high fiber content will improve its degradability up to 50 %.

Table 4.7 Selected reports on wet anaerobic digestion of solid waste as comparison to anaerobic digestion of press water

Source of solid waste	TS of substrate (%)	Type of process	HRT (days)	OLR [VS] (kg·m⁻³·d⁻¹)	VS removal (%)	CH₄ yield [VS added] (m³·kg⁻¹)	CH₄ prod. rate (m³·m⁻³·d⁻¹)	Author(s)
Milled fresh OFMSW	10	· Laboratory-scale digester, fed batchwise with controlled pH · Volume of the reactors: 6 L · Mesophilic (36 °C)	12	5.0	50	0.30[a]	1.50	Kryztek et al., 2001
Source sorted OFMSW	5	· Laboratory-scale digester · Volume of the reactor: 35 L connected with 77 L of gas collector · Thermophilic (55 °C)	15	2.8	81	0.27 0.41	0.70-1.15	Davidsson et al., 2007
Two-phase olive mill solid residue	14.3	· Laboratory-scale digester · Volume of the reactor: 2.0 L · Mesophilic (35 °C)	24 20 17	5.3 6.5 7.2	88 85 83	0.26 0.26 0.24	1.39 1.68 1.70	Rincón et al., 2008
Slaughterhouse waste, manure, market waste	4.5 6.9	· Laboratory-scale digester · Volume of the reactor: 1.8 L · Mesophilic (35 °C)	30	1.31 2.03	52 52	0.32 0.26	0.42 0.53	Alvarez and Lidén, 2008
Mixture of fruit & vegetable wastes	6.4	· Laboratory-scale/two-stage system · Volume of the reactors: 1.3 L (1ˢᵗ phase), 5.0 L (2ⁿᵈ phase) · Mesophilic (35 °C)	17.9 9.0 6.0 4.5	3.1 6.3 9.4 12.6	72 53 38 27	0.46 0.24 0.12 0.05	1.42 1.53 1.09 0.69	Mtz.– Viturtia et al., 1995
Sieved grey waste (contained 60-70 % VS)	7.0 6.3 9.4	· Laboratory-scale/two-stage system · Volume of the reactors: 2.5 L (1ˢᵗ phase), 58.5 L (2ⁿᵈ phase) · Thermophilic (60-70 °C for 1ˢᵗ phase, 55 °C for 2ⁿᵈ phase)	14.2 14.2 14.2	3.3 4.3 6.1	76.4 79.6 77.4	0.32 0.38 0.32	1.06 1.63 1.95	Scherer et al., 2000
Fruit and vegetable wastes	10	· Laboratory-scale/two-stage system · Volume of the reactors: 1.5 L (1ˢᵗ phase), 5.0 L (2ⁿᵈ phase) · Mesophilic (35 °C)	ca.13	5.5 7.4	n.a n.a	0.23 0.23	0.41 0.41	Bouallagui et al., 2004

Table 4.7 Selected reports on wet anaerobic digestion of solid waste as comparison to anaerobic digestion of press water (cont.)

Source of solid waste	TS of substrate (%)	Type of process	HRT (days)	OLR [VS] (kg·m⁻³·d⁻¹)	VS removal (%)	CH₄ yield [VSadded] (m³·kg⁻¹)	CH₄ prod. rate (m³·m⁻³·d⁻¹)	Author(s)
Source sorted OFMSW (excluding garden waste)	6	· Laboratory-scale/two-stage system · Volume of the reactors: 3.5 L (1st phase), 1 L (2nd phase) · Thermophilic (55 °C, 1st phase), hyperthermophilic (68 °C, 2nd phase)	22 18 18	2.3 3.0 3.4	78 80 82	0.48 0.41 0.44	1.12 1.23 1.50	Hartmann and Ahring, 2005
Pre-composted mechanically-sorted OFMSW	16	· Pilot-scale digester · Volume of the reactor: 3 m³ · Thermophilic (55 °C)	14.6 11.7	5.9 6.9	48 43	0.27 0.27	1.53 1.74	Checchi et al., 1991
Mixture of OFMSW, food waste and rumen	< 15	· Full-scale BTA digester · Capacity of the digester: 15 kt/year · Mesophilic (n.a.)	15.4 14.6 10.5 7.4	3.0 3.7 5.4 5.4	54 64 48 47	0.29 0.34 0.25 0.27	0.87 1.26 1.35 1.46	Kübler et al., 2000
Mechanically separated OFMSW	12	· Full-scale Vagron/Waasa process · Volume of the reactors: 4 x 2,750 m³ · Mesophilic (35 °C)	18	7.7	60-69	0.38-0.50	3.13	Luning et al., 2003
Source-sorted OFMSW	7.6-8.5	· Laboratory-scale digester · Volume of the reactor: 8.5 L · Mesophilic (37 °C)	20 10 5.7	2.6ᵇ 5.2ᵇ 10.3ᵇ	n.a. n.a. n.a.	0.43 0.40ᶜ 0.40	1.13 2.08ᶜ 4.14	Gallert et al., 2003
		· Full-scale BTA digester · Volume of the reactor: 1350 m³ · Mesophilic (37 °C)	12	5.6ᵇ	n.a.	0.30– 0.33	1.69-1.82	

n.a : data not available

[a] : assumed that CH₄ content was 60 %

[b] : calculated by regression value of COD and VS of the feeding substrate

[c] : assumed that CH₄ content was 65 %

4.2.8   Energy recovery from anaerobic digestion of press water

Table 4.5 presents a rough preliminary calculation of the anaerobic reactor dimension in a composting plant equipped with pressing facility. The energy balance with energy gain from biogas and energy requirement for substrate pre-treatment and maintenance of anaerobic digestion is also presented in the table. The analysis is calculated using the composting plant in Grünstadt, Rhineland-Palatinate as an example. Based on the experience in this composting plant, one ton of delivered OFMSW typically resu ted in 0.7 ton of solid-state waste and 0.3 ton of press water. This composting plant generates approximately 40 m^3 of press water daily. To prevent a problem caused by massive foaming at an OLR higher than 21.3 kg COD $\cdot$ m^{-3} $\cdot$ d^{-1}, HRT of 10 days is considered as optimum. Furthermore, this designated HRT ensures the organic matter removal efficiency and a reserve capacity for shock loading (safety factor) or for treatment of an increased amount of press water in the future. With these assumptions, a relatively small anaerobic digester (400 m^3 of active volume) can be applied.

The installation of anaerobic digester to treat press water in a composting plant seems to be advantageous in term of an energy balance. While composting is considered as an energy consuming process (around 30-35 kWh is consumed per ton of solid waste input), anaerobic digestion is a net energy producing process (typically 100 – 150 kWh per ton of input waste). The methane recovered from anaerobic digestion can be used to generate electricity for the operation of the whole composting plant and anaerobic digester (including energy consumption for pre-treatment, composting process and heating of anaerobic digester). Although the size of the anaerobic digester is relatively small, a potential benefit of around 0.5 million Euros /year can be expected from the methane recovery. Overall, about 16 % (10.8 kWh) of the energy of the biogas from press water resulted from each ton OFMSW delivered may be obtained as a net surplus energy.

Table 4.8 Energy balance, reactor volume design and potential energy recovery

Parameter	Unit	Value	Remarks
Reactor volume design and potential energy recovery:			
Press water production	$m^3 \cdot d^{-1}$	40	
Designed HRT	days	10	
Active reactor volume	m^3	400	
Daily methane production	$m^3 \cdot d^{-1}$	2,050	· 1 m^3 CH_4 = 31.46 MJ
Energy recovered	$kWh \cdot d^{-1}$	7,174	(at 37 °C)
			· 1 MJ = 0.278 kWh
Potential benefit	€/year	497,543	· generator efficiency = 40%
			· 1 kWh = 0.19 Euro
Energy balance in the composting plant (pro ton OFMSW delivered):			
Energy recovered from press water	kWh	71.7	
Energy for composting	kWh	21.0	35 kWh pro ton OFMSW input (Hartmann and Ahring, 2006)
Energy for AD processes (pre-treatment and pumping)	kWh	28.7	40% of energy produced (Murphy and McKeogh, 2004)
Energy for AD heating	kWh	7.2	10% of energy produced-as electricity (Murphy and McKeogh, 2004)
Surplus energy	kWh	14.8	

4.3 Anaerobic co-digestion of biowaste with press water and foodwaste for the improvement of biogas production

Energy is considered as one of the driving forces for economic and social development. Therefore, the availability of energy in a sufficient and sustainable amount has been becoming world's main interest. However, depending on the way the energy is produced, distributed, and used, it may contribute to environmental problems such as water and air pollution or even global climate change. To alleviate such negative impacts, one important political goal of most industrialized nations has been the reduction of the energy-based environmental pollution. In this context, renewable sources of energy seem to be an alternative option to improve the environmental situation by taking advantage of other additional positive effects.

In Europe for instance, the European Council has set targets regarding the use of renewable energy sources. The council targeted that in 2020 the contribution of renewable energies to be 20% of the total energy consumption and a minimum of 10% of the total consumption of gasoline and diesel for transport (EC, 2009). To promote the use and development of energy from renewable resources, different policies have been established within EU member states such as energy pricing measures (allowing manufacturers of renewable energy to sell their products at a premium price), investment subsidies and defined energy source quota obligations, *i.e.* under defined conditions, a certain share of energy must be produced from renewable resources (DMEE, 1996, Kaltschmitt and Weber, 2006)

One potential source of renewable energy is biomass including solid wastes from agriculture, food processing, and municipal activities. Among the technologies available for the treatment of municipal solid waste, anaerobic digestion is a well-known and reliable technology to treat and convert organic solid wastes to methane for energy production as part of municipal policies for the reduction of green house gas emissions. Therefore, concerning the increase of energy demand and the high masses of organic solid waste, anaerobic digestion could play an important role in dealing with those problems. However, due to financial and operation regulation reasons, the construction of new anaerobic digesters is not always possible. Optimizing the existing anaerobic digesters treating OFMSW by means of co-digestion with other types of wastes can be considered as a strategy to maximize the renewable energy production and at the same time also optimizing the organic municipal solid waste management. Moreover, the improvement of biogas production makes the operation of anaerobic digesters more economically feasible (Ahring *et al.*, 1992).

Co-digestion of solid waste with other waste streams offers several advantages such as improvement of biogas yield due to positive synergisms established in the digestion medium, improvement of process stability and better handling of mixed waste streams (Mata-Alvarez *et al.* 2000). The balance of nutrients, an appropriate C/N ratio and a stable pH are prerequisites for a stable process performance in an anaerobic digester. The optimization of the carbon to nitrogen ratio during a co-digestion process for instance, was reported to be beneficial to the methane yield (Sonowski *et al.*, 2003). The addition of inorganic compounds to some organic waste types, such as clays and iron compounds, have been reported to counteract the inhibitory effect of ammonia and sulfide, respectively (Hartmann *et al.* 2003). Mhsandete *et al.* (2004) also reported that an improvement of the buffer capacity was resulting and can be considered as one advantage of co-digestion process. However, a random or careless decision on the type of wastes that can be used as co-substrate (in regard with their specific characteristics) and the ratio between the waste streams to full-scale anaerobic digesters often lead to the process upset and significant reduction of biogas production (Murto *et al.*, 2004, Zaher *et al*, 2009).

The aim of this sub-chapter study was to examine the suitability of press water and foodwaste as co-substrates in anaerobic digestion of biowaste, judging by the performance of the reactor (*i.e.* there is no negative impacts and significant improvement of biogas production during co-digestion process). The OLR increase by addition of co-substrates was also evaluated in order to determine the optimum ratio between the main substrate and co-substrates.

4.3.1   Loading regime of the laboratory-scale reactor

Table 4.9 presents the main characteristics (COD, solids content and methane production potential) of the substrates during the anaerobic co-digestion experiments. More comprehensive details of the characteristics of the substrates can be found in sub-chapter 4.1 and 4.2. The COD and solids content of the biowaste suspension varied due to different sampling dates used in this study while the COD and solids content of press water and foodwaste were considered to be constant since the samples of both substrates were taken only once and stored in a refrigerator.

Table 4.9 Main characteristics of substrates for anaerobic co-digestion experiment

Characteristic	Unit	Biowaste	Foodwaste	Press water
COD_{total}	$g \cdot L^{-1}$	98-107	350	213
$COD_{soluble}$	$g \cdot L^{-1}$	36-36.4	120	100
Total solids (TS)	$g \cdot L^{-1}$	65-86	255	168
Volatile solids (VS)	$g \cdot L^{-1}$	53-64	225	118
CH_4 prod. potential	$m^3 \cdot kg^{-1}$ VS	0.37	0.52	0.49

One notable disadvantage of anaerobic digestion for solid waste treatment is the relatively long time requirements of the start-up period, a condition attributed to the slow growth rates of anaerobic bacteria. Several reports indicated that a steady-state condition in laboratory or full-scale digesters required a long period of start-up ranging from three weeks to one year (Maroun and El Fadel, 2007). Several strategies to obtain faster and successful start-up periods have been reported. Angelidaki et al. (2006) for example, reported that using digested manure as inoculum and applying a progressive-rate-increasing feeding gave a better result compared to constant-rate feeding. In order to shorten the start-up period, the reactor was fully filled with the sieved effluent from the full-scale biowaste reactor of Karlsruhe-Durlach. By applying this strategy, the steady-state condition of the reactor at a designated OLR can be achieved in less than 3 weeks and the results (i.e. biogas production and organic matters elimination) could be used as the reference. Therefore, compared to the previous studies on anaerobic digestion of solid waste, the start-up period of this experiment was relatively short.

The variation of HRTs and their relationship with the increment of OLRs during the experiment are plotted in Figure 4.18. For this study, the experiment using laboratory-scale reactor was carried out in three steps for about seven months. To simulate the operation of the full-scale biowaste reactor in Karlsruhe-Durlach, the reactor was only fed during the working days (Monday to Friday). The feeding was done twice a day (i.e. 9.00 a.m. and 16.00 p.m.) in semi-continuous feeding mode. The feeding of the reactor was fixed with 1.0 L of biowaste suspension per day throughout the whole experiment. In the first step, to be able to evaluate the improvement of biogas production rate by the addition of press water and foodwaste, the reactor was initially fed with biowaste suspensions only at an OLR of 12.3 kg $COD \cdot m^{-3} \cdot d^{-1}$ (HRT= 8 days). After the steady-state condition in the first step was reached, the OLR was then increased step-wise by means of press water and foodwaste addition to a final OLR of 20.1 kg COD $\cdot$ m^{-3} $\cdot$ d^{-1} during co-digestion with press water (the second step: week 4 to week 17) and to 22.0 kg COD$\cdot$m$^{-3}\cdot$d^{-1} during co-digestion with foodwaste (the third step: 18 to week 30).

The increment of the OLR was initially done by adding 50 mL of press water to the biowaste suspension. After a steady-state condition was reached, the volume of press water was increased again by 50 mL press water addition per increment to a maximum addition of 250 mL (25 % of the biowaste suspension by volume). The addition of press water as co-substrate caused a reduction of the HRT from 8 days to 6.4 days. A similar procedure of co-substrate addition was also applied during co-digestion with foodwaste. However, due to insignificant biogas production improvement and poor performance of the reactor in converting fatty acids to methane (see also Figure 4.20 and 4.21), the addition substrate with 200 mL of foodwaste (20% of biowaste suspension by volume) was considered as maximum. With this addition the HRT of the reactor reached 6.7 days.

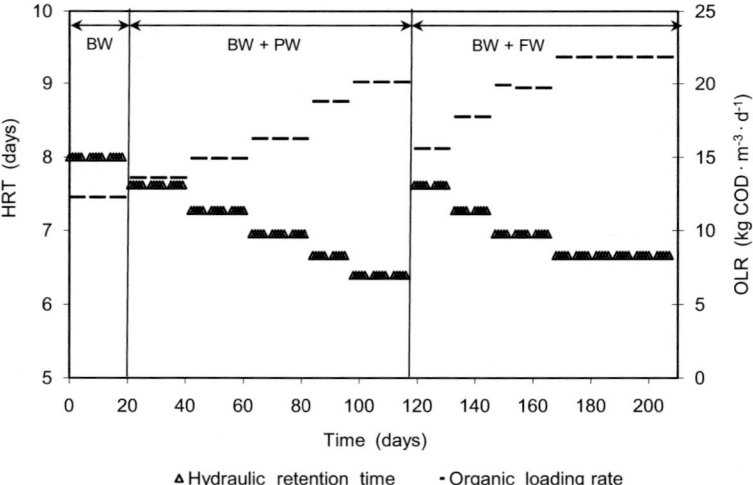

Figure 4.18 Loading regime during the co-digestion experiment (BW: biowaste suspension, PW: press water and FW: foodwaste)

4.3.2   Biogas production

Figure 4.19 depicts the variations of daily biogas and methane production rates at different OLR during the co-digestion experiment. Similar as in the full-scale biowaste digester in Karlsruhe-Durlach and as in previous studies (sub-chapter 4.1 and 4 2) the daily biogas production fluctuated due to a deficiency of fresh substrate during no-feeding period in the weekends. During a week of operation, the biogas production rate reached its maximum value after the 3rd day of a week (Wednesday) and the value was relatively stable on the next days.

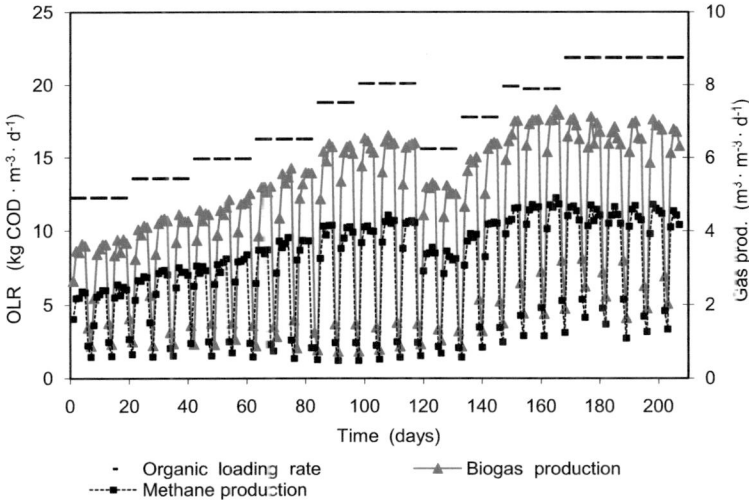

Figure 4.19 The variations of daily volumetric biogas and methane production at different OLR during the co-digestion experiments.

To obtain an idea about the increase of biogas due to the addition of co-substrates, the step-wise increments of the OLR and their relationship with the biogas production rates are presented in Figure 4.20 while the quantitative values are presented in Table 4.10. The biogas production rates presented were the average values of biogas production rates in the last three days of a week (Wednesday, Thursday and Friday) when the biogas production was considered stable. The blue solid circle is the average biogas production rate from the reactor when it was fed with biowaste suspension only. This value, considering also its OLR value in terms of the COD loading rate, is used as the reference. From the figure, it is shown that the biogas production within the same range of OLR increment, from co-digestion with foodwaste was higher as compared to the co-digestion with press water. However, an addition of foodwaste which resulted in an OLR of more than 17.5 kg $COD \cdot m^{-3} \cdot d^{-1}$ gave no significant biogas increase and even slightly dropped when the OLR was increased to 21.9 kg $COD \cdot m^{-3} \cdot d^{-1}$.

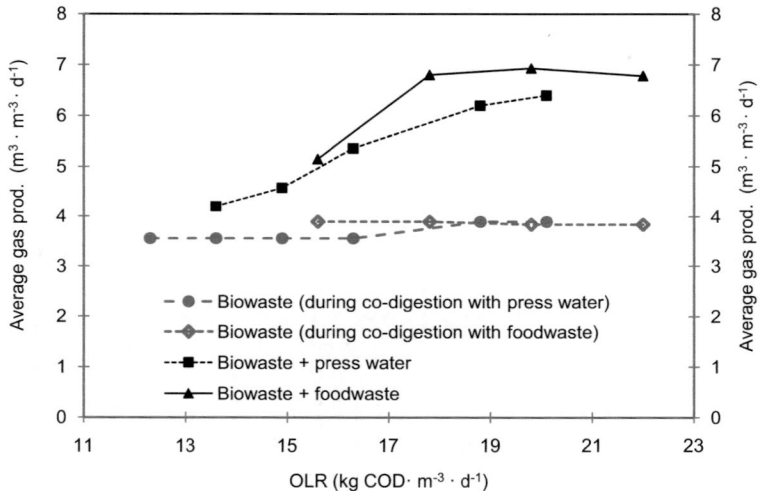

Figure 4.20 The average biogas production rate at different OLR during the co-digestion experiments.

From Table 4.10 it can be seen that the addition of a co-substrate not only increased the biogas production rate linearly with the increment of OLRs but also improved the biogas production rate. For instance, an increment of the OLR by 10.9 % during co-digestion with press water (compared to the OLR by biowaste suspension only) increased the biogas production rate as much as 18.3%. During the co-digestion with press water, the maximum biogas production improvement was reached when the addition of press water was 20 % of the volume of biowaste suspension (19.7 % improvement). The improvement of biogas production was only 14.9 % when the OLR was increased by 49.6 % through addition of 25 % press water.

Tabel 4.10 Average values of biogas production after increasing the OLR by co-substrate addition

Week	Substrate	Co-substrate addition (L · d⁻¹)	HRT (days)	OLR [COD] (kg · m⁻³ · d⁻¹)	Additional OLR[*] (%)	Biogas prod. rate (m³ · m⁻³ · d⁻¹)	Methane content (%)	Biogas prod. improvement[**] (%)
1-3	Biowaste	-	8.0	12.3	-	3.56	65.2	-
4-6		+ 0.05	7.6	13.6	10.9	4.20	66.8	18.3
7-9	Biowaste + press water	+ 0.10	7.3	14.9	21.8	4.58	66.9	29.0
10-12		+ 0.15	7.0	16.3	32.6	5.36	66.8	51.0
13-14		+ 0.20	6.7	18.8	39.7	6.20	65.5	59.4
15-17		+ 0.25	6.4	20.1	49.6	6.40	65.7	64.6
18-19		+ 0.05	7.6	15.6	16.0	5.15	65.7	32.4
20-21	Biowaste + foodwaste	+ 0.10	7.3	17.8	32.1	6.08	66.0	56.3
22-24		+ 0.15	7.0	19.7	48.8	6.93	66.1	80.7
25-30		+ 0.20	6.7	21.9	65.1	6.78	66.5	76.8

[*] : considering only additional OLR from press water and foodwaste (not total additional OLR from initial OLR of biowaste-only feeding)

[**] : considering only biogas production improvement caused by additional COD from press water and foodwaste

The biogas production increased to 80.7% compared to the reference value when the OLR was increased by 48.8% during co-digestion with foodwaste at 15 % volume addition. Therefore, a net biogas production improvement of 31.9 % was achieved. This value was considered the maximum since the addition of foodwaste at 20% volume only gave a net biogas improvement of 14.9% and the performance of the reactor was considered as deteriorated. There was a slight methane content improvement during co-digestion with press water and foodwaste compared to the methane content during the feeding with biowaste suspension only. The methane content of the biogas reached an average of 65 to 67 % and was stable at this range throughout the experiment.

Considering the methane production potential of the substrates, the substrates used in this study can be considered as readily degradable. From the calculation using the results during the batch tests for methane production (see also sub-chapter 4.1 and 4.2), 80% of the maximum methane production potential, was reached in only 1.6 days. To achieve the same level of degradation, press water and foodwaste needed 2.6 days and 3.8 days, respectively. The addition of foodwaste gave more biogas, most probably due to its higher content of lipids. As has been discussed also in sub-chapter 4.1.2, lipids may potentially produce almost double as much biogas compared to carbohydrates or proteins.

Several authors also reported that the biogas productivity of anaerobic digesters can be improved by supplementing the main substrate with readily digestible co-substrates. Fontoulakis and Manios (2009) for instance, reported about the possibility to use crude glycerol, which is a major by-product of biodiesel production, as a co-substrate in anaerobic digestion of OFMSW. The authors noted that by the addition of crude glycerol, the methane production in a reactor treating the OFMSW increased almost by 50%. Bouallagui et al. (2009) observed that the addition of abattoir wastewater and waste activated sludge to an anaerobic digestion of fruit and vegetable solid waste with a ratio of 10% (w/w VS) enhanced the biogas yield by 51.5% and 43.8% and total volatile solids removal by 10% and 11.7%, respectively. The co-digestion of a simulated OFMSW with fats of animal and vegetable origin has been reported to increase the amount of biogas produced according to the applied organic loading rate. Although the yields of biogas generated per kg VS degraded were similar to those found with OFMSW only, the methane content in the biogas produced was higher in the presence of fats (Fernáncez et al., 2005).

4.3.3 Volatile fatty acid residues in the effluent

Figure 4.21 depicts the residual volatile fatty acids concentration in the digestate of the reactor. Of four different volat le fatty acids (acetate, propionate, butyrate and valeriate) measured in this study, butyrate and valeriate were detected in insignificant amounts or even could not be detected. Therefore, only the concentrations of acetate and propionate were considered as important throughout this study. The absence of butyrate and valeriate was probably due to either not being produced as intermediate products or to their acetogenic conversion to acetate and hydrogen, which proceeded were much faster at any time than their generation (Gallert and Winter, 2005).

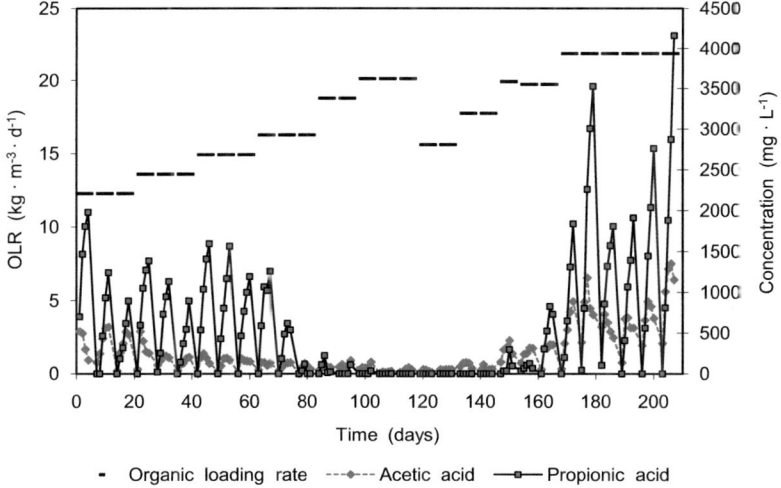

Figure 4.21 Variation of residual volatile fatty acid concentrations in the reactor's effluent at different OLR during co-digestion experiment.

In the first week during start-up phase, propionate concentration accumulated and its concentration increased to around 2,000 mg·L^{-1}. However, this relatively high propionate concentration seemed not to inhibit the biogas production or to influence the overall anaerobic process. The process was considered as relatively stable indicated by the constant value of pH, high COD elimination and reasonable biogas production. The propionate decreased to zero after the weekends (measured on Mondays) and started to increase again due to the fresh feeding or after the increment of the OLR. However, the peak concentration never exceeded 2,000 mg·L^{-1} and tended to have lower peak concentrations in the following weeks. Unlike propionate, the initially produced-concentration of acetate was immediately degraded. Only a low concentration of acetate was found in the digestate after a no-feeding period during weekends. Although the concentration of acetate started to increase when the fresh feeding was introduced, in the first three weeks of the operation the maximum concentration was lower than 500 mg·L^{-1}.

After 12 weeks of operation at an OLR of 16.3 kg COD·m^{-3}·d^{-1} (during co-digestion with 15% press water addition), the concentration of propionate started to decrease to a non-measurable concentration, indicating that the activity of propionate-degraders within the group of acetogenic bacteria had adapted to the organic loading and co-digestion condition. Residual acetate was still found but in a low concentration of less than 150 mg·L^{-1}. This condition (low concentration of residual acetate and propionate) continued to occur during co-digestion with press water until the OLR was increased to 20.1 kg COD·m^{-3}·d^{-1} (25% press water addition). When the co-substrate was changed to foodwaste (up to 10% foodwaste addition), this condition was also found.

The concentration of both volatile acids started to increase when the OLR reached 19.7 kg COD·m^{-3}·d^{-1} (15% addition of foodwaste). During the feeding at this OLR, the concentration of acetate and propionate increased to a maximum value of 400 mg·L^{-1} and 830 mg·L^{-1}, respectively. However, the reactor did not show any decrease in the performance and even the biogas production improved significantly (see Table 4.10). When the addition foodwaste was increased to 20% of the biowaste suspension volume, acetate and propionate concentration increased to more than 1,000 mg·L^{-1} and 3,500 mg·L^{-1}, respectively. In order to give more adaptation time to the sludge of the reactor, the feeding was maintained at the same OLR for 6 weeks. However, the concentration of both volatile acids did not tend to decrease except after weekends. Although a high concentration of fatty acids, a slight decrease of the pH value (never dropped to below 7.0) and a higher soluble COD (see also Table 4.12 for pH and soluble COD values) were observed in the effluent, in general the reactor did not show any irreversible failure. There was an increase of biogas production although the net biogas improvement was lower compared to that of 15% addition of foodwaste.

Available reports regarding the inhibition effect of volatile acids are sometimes contradicting each other. For instance, although some authors (*e.g.* McCarty and Brosseau, 1963 in Vavilin *et al.*, 2003) reported that methanogenic bacteria were inhibited at propionate concentration of 1000 mg·L^{-1}, Gallert and Winter (2008) reported that during a restart of a full-scale anaerobic digester, a maximum propionate concentration of 6,200 mg·L^{-1} was accumulated and the restart still could proceed successfully. Thus, it can be concluded that as long as the pH value of the digestate is maintained at the range suitable for anaerobic digestion processes (minimum value of 6.8) the accumulation of propionate at high concentration can be tolerated.

4.3.4 COD and solids elimination

The efficiency of the reactor to reduce organic compounds was measured daily by determining the elimination of total COD. When steady-state conditions at each co-digestion step were reached, total solids and volatile solids of the reactor effluent were also measured in order to examine the solids removal efficiency. Figure 4.22 presents the daily COD elimination efficiency at different OLR levels caused by different ratio and type of co-substrates.

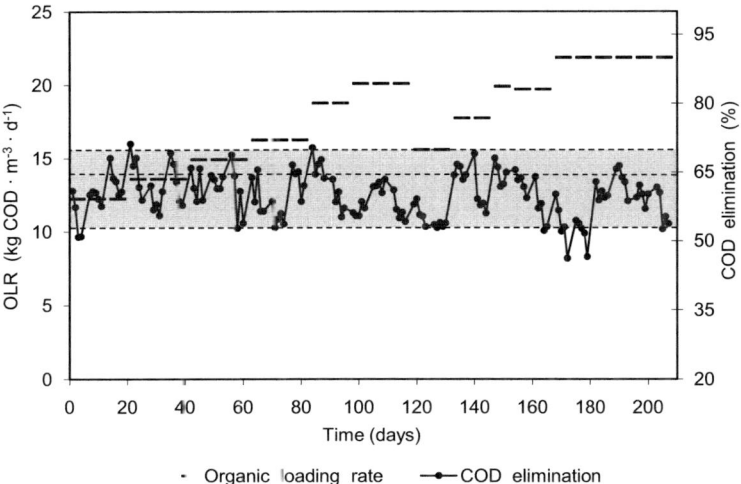

Figure 4.22 OLR and COD elimination efficiency during co-digestion experiment.

At all level of OLRs, the total COD elimination was relatively stable in the range of 53 – 70% (with an average value of 60%). During the feeding from Monday to Friday, the highest COD elimination was measured on every Monday since there was no fresh feeding in the weekend. The COD elimination decreased to lower than 50% when the feeding of the reactor was increased to an OLR of 21.9 kg $COD \cdot m^{-3} \cdot d^{-1}$ by co-digestion with 20% foodwaste addition. However, after two weeks the COD elimination increased to the already mentioned range.

Table 4.11 presents the solids and COD removal efficiency of the reactor related to its OLRs (in term of VS loading) and methane yields. The elimination of TS and VS ranged from 37% to 50% and 47% to 57%, respectively. During co-digestion with press water, the elimination of TS and VS was relatively stable and had irrelevant difference compared to the value of solids elimination when the reactor was fed with biowaste only. A decrease of solids elimination efficiencies was observed when the co-substrate was changed to foodwaste. During the co-digestion with foodwaste, TS removal only reached 37% to 41% which meant a decrease of around 13% to 20% compared to the level of TS elimination during the feeding with biowaste only. The elimination of VS also showed a decrease of about 9% to 16%. However, the VS elimination during co-digestion with both co-substrates was still considered as acceptable in practice. Kübler et al. (2000) reported that anaerobic digestion in a full-scale BTA process using substrate of a mixture of OFMSW, foodwaste and animal rumen resulted in a VS elimination ranging from 47% to 64% and a methane yield ranging from $0.27 – 0.34 \text{ m}^3 \cdot kg^{-1} \text{ VS}_{added}$. However, the OLRs applied by the authors were far lower those that used in this study ($3.0 – 5.4 \text{ kg VS} \cdot m^{-3} \cdot d^{-1}$ by Kübler et al. and $6.8 – 12.3 \text{ kg VS} \cdot m^{-3} \cdot d^{-1}$ in this study).

The methane yield during co-digestion with foodwaste did not decrease although the solids elimination was deteriotrated. This was probably due to the higher content of lipids in foodwaste. Compared to the previous reports about anaerobic digestion of solid waste, especially on wet anaerobic digestion systems, the methane yields of this study was relatively high (see also Table 4.7, sub-chapter 4.2).

Table 4.11 Average values of organic matters degradation and methane yield during the co-digestion experiments (in biowaste and biowaste plus either press water or foodwaste)

Week	Substrate	OLR [VS] (kg·m⁻³·d⁻¹)	Avg. TS elimination (%)	Avg. VS elimination (%)	Avg. COD elimination (%)	Methane yield (m³·kg⁻¹ VS)	Methane prod. rate (m³·m⁻³·d⁻¹)
1-3	Biowaste	6.76	46.8	55.6	59.6	0.34	2.32
4-6		7.50	47.4	52.3	62.3	0.37	2.81
7-9		8.23	46.5	54.9	61.7	0.37	3.06
10-12	Biowaste + press water	8.97	44.2	52.5	59.6	0.40	3.58
13-14		11.01	49.7	56.5	62.8	0.37	4.06
15-17		11.74	46.2	55.2	58.5	0.36	4.20
18-19		9.47	40.8	50.5	54.9	0.36	3.38
20-21	Biowaste + foodwaste	10.88	37.1	46.7	62.5	0.37	4.01
22-24		10.91	37.8	48.3	61.5	0.42	4.58
25-30		12.31	40.6	50.0	57.7	0.37	4.51

4.3.5   Other characteristics of the effluent

During the co-digestion experiment, some parameters such as acid capacity (Ger.: *Säurekapazität*), ammonia nitrogen and soluble COD of the effluent were also measured. Acid capacity is a measure for the buffer capacity of a liquid waste against acids and thus responsible for pH value stability. The acid capacity of the reactor's effluent was proceeded by measuring how much acid - in this study 0.5 $mol·L^{-1}$ hydrochloric acid (HCl) - is necessary by a defined quantity of liquid sample to adjust the pH value to 4.3. The typical curve of the pH value an acid capacity test is depicted in Figure 4.23. From this figure, it can be seen that the pH did not decrease linearly according to the addition of hydrochloric acid, but there was a buffering mechanisms that prevented the pH value to continuously drop (*i.e.* within the decrease range of 6.5 to 5.5). As presented in Table 4.12, the acid capacity of the reactor increased when the biowaste as the main substrate was supplied with press water or foodwaste. This leads to the conclusion that the addition of both co-substrates improved the buffering capacity of the reactor.

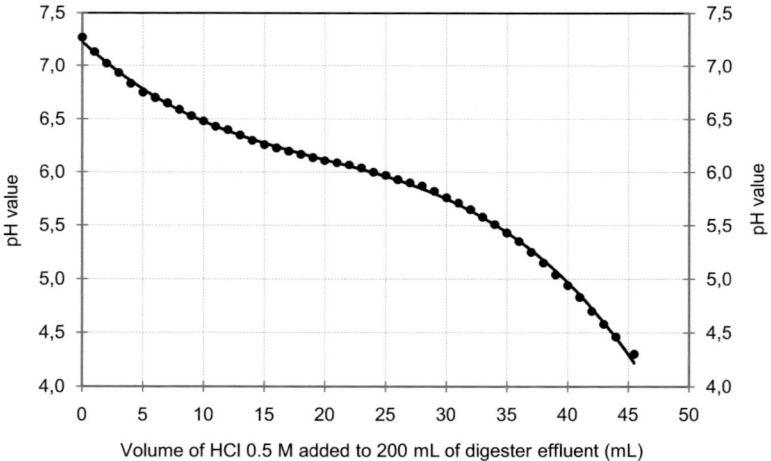

Figure 4.23 Typical curve of pH value during an acid capacity test (plotted in this graph was the test using the effluent of the reactor when it was fed with 1 L of biowaste).

High buffering capacity of a digester is an important factor for a successful anaerobic digestion process. In some case, due to a lower buffer capacity, a specific substrate is difficult to be degraded. Angelidaki and Ahring (1997) for instance, reported that oil mill effluent waste (OME) has to be diluted before it would be fed to anaerobic digester since it was quite difficult to be degraded. By co-digestion with animal manure, it was shown that the high buffering capacity contained in manure, together with the content of several essential nutrients, make it possible to degrade OME without previous dilution, without addition of external alkalinity and without addition of external nitrogen source.

Soluble COD of the reactor's effluent, which can be considered as the COD of wastewater produced by the anaerobic digestion system is also presented in Table 4.12. During co-digestion with 25% addition of press water to 10% addition of foodwaste, the value of soluble COD was relatively low, even compared to the value when the reactor was fed with biowaste only. This is explained by the low concentration of residual fatty acids in that range of feeding period. However, the soluble COD of the effluent increased to a maximum value of 15.1 $g \cdot L^{-1}$ with an average value of 8.7 $g \cdot L^{-1}$ when the feeding was supplemented with 20% of foodwaste. At the same time, the concentrations of acetate and propionate were also high. Thus, it can be concluded that the concentration of soluble COD was related to the concentration of fatty acids as residual from acetogenesis and acidogenesis products which cannot be completely converted to the final product (biogas). Therefore, the soluble COD can also be used as a tool to examine whether an aerobic digester performs well or not.

According to Graja and Wilderer (2001), the net amount of wastewater produced by anaerobic digesters depended on various parameters, such as the water content of the incoming biowaste (determining the amount of process water that has to be recycled), the amount of water lost during pretreatment, the amount of moisture produced during the digestion and the performance of the solid-liquid separation device of the effluent (*i.e.* centrifuge). Kübler (1996) estimated that an average volume of roughly of 500 L of wastewater eventually leaves the anaerobic digestion system per ton of biowaste delivered. Therefore, soluble COD is also an important parameter since the effluent of an anaerobic digester after centrifugation will result in a huge amount of wastewater which needs further treatment. The higher the concentration of soluble COD, the more costly is the treatment of wastewater.

Table 4.12 Soluble COD, pH, ammonia and acid capacity of the reactor's effluent

Week to:	Substrate(s)	Soluble COD ($g \cdot L^{-1}$)	pH (-)	NH_4^+-N ($mg \cdot L^{-1}$)	$KS_{4.3}$ ($mmol \cdot L^{-1}$)
1-3	1L B	3.2-6.8 (5.0)	7.1-7.3	460	113
4-6	1L B + 0.05 P	4.6-8.4 (6.4)	7.2-7.3	625	122
15-17	1L B + 0.25 P	3.0-4.7 (3.9)	7.2-7.3	609	150
18-19	1L B + 0.05 F	3.3-4.9 (4.1)	7.2-7.3	679	130
22-24	1L B + 0.10 F	4.2-6.3 (4.8)	7.2-7.2	723	145
25-30	1L B + 0.20 F	4.7-15.1 (8.7)	7.0-7.3	740	150

B: biowaste suspension, P: press water, F: foodwaste

Table 4.12 also presents the concentration of ammonium-nitrogen in the effluent. Ammonium and ammonia, which are the products of the anaerobic digestion of proteins and amino acids, are present in all anaerobic digesters treating organic waste or wastewater. Ammonium ion (NH_4^+) exists in equilibrium with free ammonia (NH_3) and hydrogen ion (H^+), as shown in the following equation:

$$NH_4^+ \leftrightarrow NH_3 + H^+$$

Lay *et al.* (1998) indicated that the ammonium nitrogen concentration was a more significant factor than the free ammonia in affecting the methanogenic activity of a well-acclimatized system. The authors also collected reports from previous studies regarding inhibition caused by ammonium. They reported that ammonium-nitrogen concentrations between 200 and 1,500 $mg \cdot L^{-1}$ were thought to have no significant adverse effects on methanogenesis. However, at concentrations exceeding 700 $mg \cdot L^{-1}$, increasing concentration resulted in decreasing methanogenic activity. They also reported that ammonium-nitrogen concentrations between 1,500 and 3,000 $mg \cdot L^{-1}$ were inhibitory at pH levels greater than 7.4, whereas the ammonium-nitrogen concentrations in excess of 3,000 $mg \cdot L^{-1}$ were expected to be toxic at all pH values.

The addition of press water and foodwaste resulted in a significant increase of ammonia-nitrogen concentrations in the effluent compared to its concentration when the reactor was fed with biowaste only. This increase was probably caused by the degradation of the higher protein content in both co-substrates (indicated by a higher TKN concentration, see chapter 4.1 and 4.2).

4.4   Potential use of potato sludge as a co-substrate in anaerobic digestion

The potato processing industries uses a large volume of water during the production processes. The activities in this industry such as washing, peeling, blanching, slicing and shredding during production of potato chips or other potato products cause a huge amount of wastewater. The wastewater generated from the processes are characterized by high organic matter load (carbohydrates, starches, proteins, vitamins, pectines and sugars) and total suspended solids (TSS) resulting in high BOD and COD (Malladi and Ingham, 1993). This highly polluted wastewater requires a treatment before it is discharged into water bodies.

Due to its high concentration of readily biodegradable compounds, the potato industry wastewater is mostly treated with various combinations of aerobic and anaerobic biological processes (Mishra et al., 2004). A combination of surface and intermittent vertical flow wetlands, lagoons, ponds and land applications have been also used as treatment methods. Although these biological treatment processes can be applied as the efficient methods to treat the potato industry wastewater, the drawbacks are the long residence periods required, which imply a huge reactor capacity to cope with the volume of the wastewater. Moreover, the microorganisms are extremely sensitive to such factors as pH, temperature and sludge washout (Kobya et al., 2006). However, since aerobic processes are considered as more effective to treat liquid waste, aerobic techniques such as activated sludge systems are still widely used to treat this type of wastewater. One disadvantage of the application of such method is the production of excess sludge in relatively huge volume.

Sludge management is considered as one of the most difficult and expensive processes in industrial or domestic wastewater treatment engineering. It is estimated that the cost of sludge management comprises approximately 35% of the capital cost and 55% of annual operation and maintenance costs of a wastewater treatment plant (Knezevic, 1995). On the other hand, sludge quantities continue to increase, but the options for sludge disposal are limited due to the more strict regulations applied to protect the environment. Therefore, the use of excess sludge resulting from aerobic treatment of potato industry wastewater (later be called potato sludge) as co-substrate in anaerobic digestion of OFMSW can be considered as a solution.

This sub-chapter presents the characteristics of the potato sludge, its methane production potential and the solids elimination potential. These results are considered important to examine the suitability of potato sludge as a co-substrate in anaerobic digestion of OFMSW.

4.4.1 Main characteristics of potato sludge

The main characteristics of potato sludge such as its density, organic matter, volatile fatty acids, total nitrogen and also its concentration of heavy metals are presented in Table 4.13.

Table 4.13 Main characteristics of potato sludge

Parameter	Unit	Value
pH	-	4.35
Density	$ton \cdot m^{-3}$	1.02
Total solids (TS)	% (w/w)	29.1 ± 0.22
Volatile solids (VS)	% TS	76.8 ± 0.14
Chemical oxygen demand (COD total)	$g \cdot g^{-1}$ TS	0.926
Soluble COD	$g \cdot g^{-1}$ TS	0.092
Total Kjeldahl nitrogen (TKN)	$g \cdot g^{-1}$ TS	0.03
Acetic acid	$mg \cdot g^{-1}$ TS	13.90
Propionic acid	$mg \cdot g^{-1}$ TS	2.84
Butyric acid	$mg \cdot g^{-1}$ TS	n.d.*
Valeric acid	$mg \cdot g^{-1}$ TS	n.d.*
Heavy metals concentration:		
Chromium	$mg \cdot g^{-1}$ TS	n.d.
Copper	$mg \cdot g^{-1}$ TS	0.20
Mangan	$mg \cdot g^{-1}$ TS	0.07
Iron	$mg \cdot g^{-1}$ TS	12.63
Cobalt	$mg \cdot g^{-1}$ TS	n.d.
Nickel	$mg \cdot g^{-1}$ TS	0.02
Cadmium	$mg \cdot g^{-1}$ TS	< 0.01
Lead	$mg \cdot g^{-1}$ TS	0.03
Zinc	$mg \cdot g^{-1}$ TS	0.03

* n.d. : not detected

From Table 4.13, it can be seen that potato sludge has a relatively high organic matter content. The volatile solids content of the sludge reached about 22 % of the total weight. The value of total COD was close to the value of TS, however soluble COD only reached 10 % of total COD. There was already a beginning acidification process, indicated by the presence of acetate and propionate in relatively high concentration.

Due to the difficulty of measuring the exact volume of potato sludge, the heavy metals concentration was presented in weight/weight TS unit. If compared to the heavy metals concentration of press water (see Table 4.5) and also considering the density of potato sludge, the heavy metals concentration of potato sludge except for iron, copper and cadmium, were lower. However, the concentration of copper and cadmium were still lower than their toxic concentration according to Konzeli-Katsiri and Kartsonas (1986).

4.4.2   Methane production potential

The methane production potential of potato sludge was examined using batch assay tests in duplicate. The tests were performed in 1 L Schott-bottles that were inoculated with anaerobic sludge from the full-scale mesophilic biowaste reactor in Karlsruhe-Durlach. For comparison, a zero control (only inoculum without additional substrate) and a positive control using glucose as the substrate were also performed.

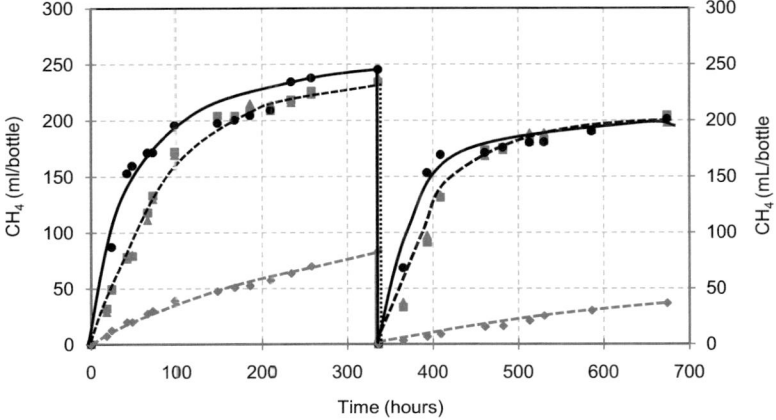

■ Potato sludge 1 (0.4 g VS/bottle)   ▲ Potato sludge 2 (0.4 g VS/bottle)
● Positive control (glucose 0.4 g VS/bottle)   ◆ Zero control (only inoculum)

Figure 4.24 Cumulative methane production during batch assay tests

The batch assay tests were performed in two feeding runs. After the methane production from the first feeding was considered in a plateau phase, the second feeding was started. In both feeding runs, the zero control still produced methane indicating that there was residual methane productivity from sludge components. However, the net methane productions of both feedings were relatively similar. Figure 4.24 shows that with the same additional amount of VS, potato sludge produced nearly the same amount of methane compared to glucose, although potato sludge needed longer time to obtain maximum methane production.

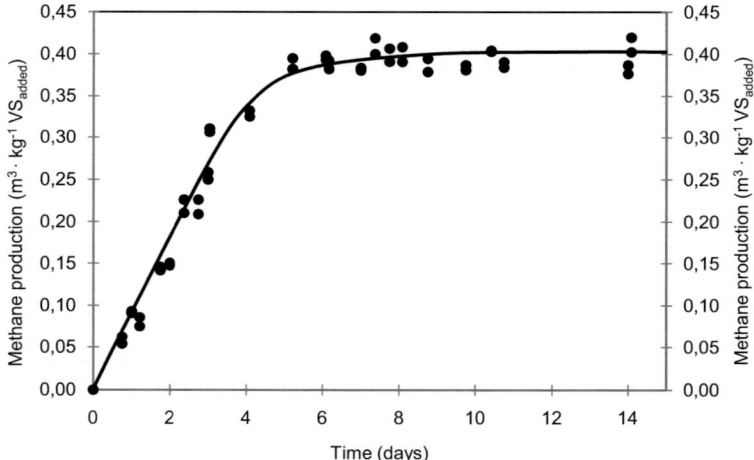

Figure 4.25 Methane production potential of potato sludge (at 37 °C).

Figure 4.25 depicts the net methane potential production of potato sludge. The curve represents methane production from potato sludge only and was obtained by subtracting methane production in assays with potato sludge addition and methane production in zero control (only inoculum sludge, without any addition of substrate). The maximum methane production potential appeared to be around 0.40 m^3 CH$_4$ · kg^{-1} VS$_{added}$ and was achieved in approximately two weeks of incubation. Compared to biowaste suspensions, potato sludge had a higher methane production potential (0.37 m^3 CH$_4$ · kg^{-1} VS$_{added}$). From Figure 4.25, potato sludge can be also considered as a readily degradable substrate. To obtain 80% of its maximum methane production potential, potato sludge only required 3.8 days of incubation. This value was comparable to the degradability grade of foodwaste (see sub-chapter 4.3).

4.4.3 Solids elimination and volatile fatty acids development

Total solids and volatile solids elimination tests were carried out using triplicate batch assays with 1.0 L Schott-bottle. The assays were inoculated with 900 mL of anaerobic sludge inoculums from the same source as for the methane production assays and 100 mL of potato sludge were added. Incubation of the assays was in a thermostated orbital shaker at 37 °C. The degraded concentrations of TS and VS and their elimination (in %) are plotted in Figure 4.26. More than 70% of the maximum elimination was achieved during the first ten days of incubation. After that, the elimination rate was slower. It was considered as not significant after 45 days. From Figure 4.26, it is shown that potato sludge had a relative good solids elimination. More than 70% of its volatile solid was eliminated, giving a TS elimination of around 50%.

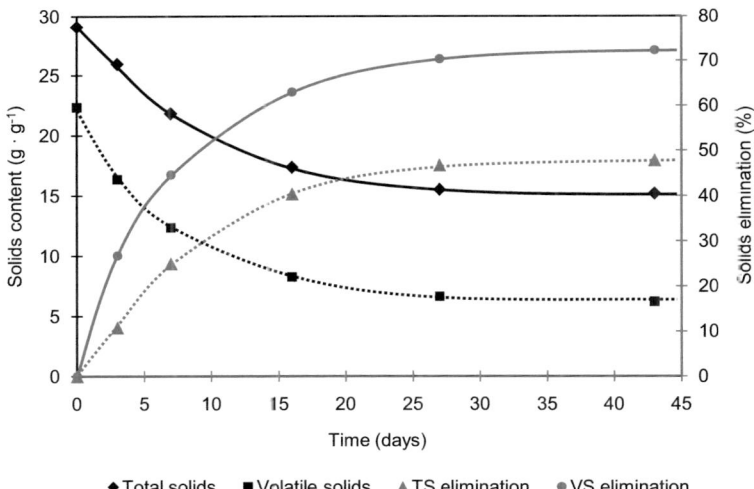

Figure 4.26 TS and VS degradation potential of potato sludge.

The concentrations of VFA in the TS and VS elimination assays were also examined daily. The development of VFA concentrations in the assays are presented in Figure 4.27. From the figure, it can be seen that acetate was produced and degraded rapidly. After reaching a maximum concentration of around 570 mg·L^{-1} in two days, acetate was rapidly degraded with a maximum degradation rate of 19.6 mg·L^{-1}· h^{-1} and completely degraded after 5 days of incubation. The accumulation of acetate was presumably due to the lack of methanogenic bacteria during "start-up" of the assays. The methanogens are generally considered to be more sensitive to environmental conditions such as low pH value or the presence of toxic substances (Lin, 1992). Moreover, the methane conversion from acetate is also known to be a rate-limiting step in methanogenesis, especially at a temperature of more than 18 °C (van Haandel *et al.*, 2005).

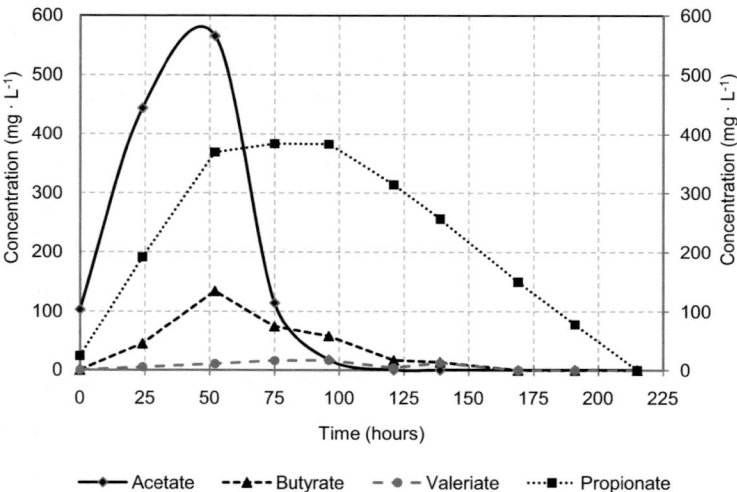

Figure 4.27 Volatile fatty acids development during solids elimination test.

The production and accumulation of propionate was also observed in the assays. The production and degradation rate of propionate was slower than that of acetate. The concentration of propionate reached its maximum value of 380 mg·L^{-1} after three days and was completely degraded after 9 days of incubation with a maximum degradation rate of propionate of 3.2 mg·L^{-1}· h^{-1}. Propionate (or other higher fatty acids) accumulated when the rate of hydrolytic and fermentative activity exceeded the rate of acetogenic conversion of fermentation of intermediates to acetate and hydrogen. It is usually produced because methanogenic bacteria cannot consume hydrogen at the rate at which it is produced (Palmisano and Barlaz, 1996).

Chapter 5

SUMMARY AND RECOMMENDATIONS

5.1   Summary

Experiments to examine the main characteristics and the biogas production potential of several biosolids were carried out in this study. Semi-continuous feeding of reactors was employed to investigate the suitability of those biosolids as a substrate or co-substrate in an anaerobic digester. From the results of the experiments during this study, several important conclusions can be drawn as follows:

The use of foodwaste as co-substrate for constant biogas supply. Source-sorted foodwaste from restaurants, hospitals, university canteens, supermarkets or catering companies have a high content of organic matter which is one of the requirements of a co-substrate. The organic matter in foodwaste was easily degradable and also had a very attractive biogas production potential. During a relatively long period of feeding with foodwaste as the sole substrate, there was no indication of an inhibitory or poisonous effect on anaerobic digestion process. The organic matter concentration of foodwaste can be adjusted to that of domestic biowaste, thus co-digestion of biowaste with foodwaste will not disturb the capacity of a biowaste plant to treat the regular biowaste volume from a city. Since the autoclaved foodwaste is perfectly homogenous, continuous addition during night time or weekends with pumps at low pumping rates without the danger of clogging and the necessity of control personnel is possible.

Figure 4.28 presents a simulation of the hourly biogas production rate in an anaerobic digester treating biowaste with and without additional foodwaste feeding. The curves were developed using the biogas production potential of biowaste and foodwaste (see Figure 4.2 and 4.3). From this figure, it can be seen that additional foodwaste feeding reduced the fluctuation of biogas production. Although there was a slight decrease in solid reduction, this result can be regarded as insignificant and is compensated by the significant increase of biogas production which consequently gives additional benefit in term of energy recovery. An additional OLR of only 23.5 % (by means of foodwaste addition) improved the daily biogas production to maximum 37 %. Therefore, it can be concluded that foodwaste can be used as co-substrate in anaerobic treatment of biowaste during night times and weekends, when no biowaste suspension is available in order to maximise or equilibrate biogas production

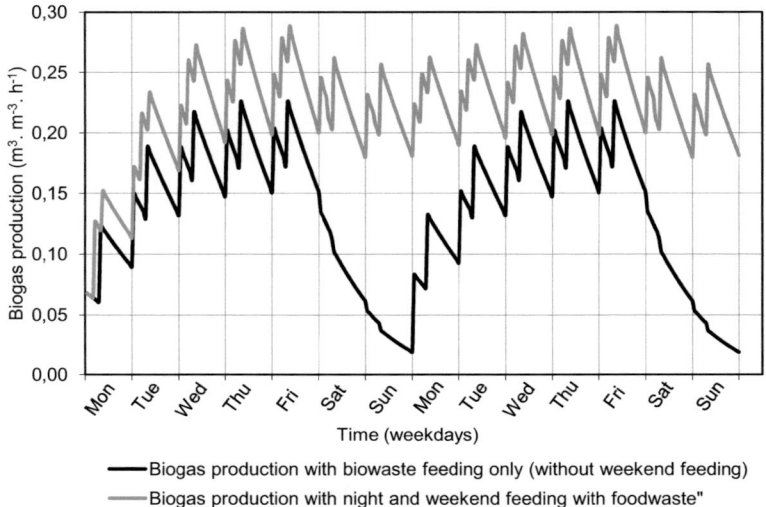

Figure 4.28 Simulation of hourly biogas production with and without additional foodwaste feeding during night and weekends.

Anaerobic digestion of press water for energy recovery. Part of the moisture content of the organic fraction of municipal solid wastes was pressed off as "press water" to reduce or avoid the necessity of addition of structural material for composting of solid residues. The press water had a high content of solubilised and fine particulate organic material and required a treatment prior to disposal. Generally, the main characteristics and methane production potential of press water classified it for use as a substrate in anaerobic digestion. Press water contains a high portion of easily degradable organic matter. The maximum methane production potential was approximately 0.27 m^3 $CH_4 \cdot kg^{-1}$ COD_{added} corresponding to 0.49 m^3 $CH_4 \cdot kg^{-1}$ VS_{added}. Almost all of the heavy metals required for an anaerobic digestion process were present in press water with concentrations lower than inhibitory or toxic.

In order to test the stability of press water as substrate in an anaerobic digester, a semi-continuously fed CSTR laboratory column reactor was run for 5 months. A stable maximal OLR of 27.7 kg COD $\cdot$ $m^{-3} \cdot d^{-1}$ (15.3 kg VS $\cdot$ $m^{-3} \cdot d^{-1}$) could be reached, which is a relatively high loading compared to other anaerobic digesters treating OFMSW. The specific biogas yield was relatively stable at values between 0.647 m^3-biogas $\cdot$ kg^{-1} VS and 0.696 m^3 biogas $\cdot$ kg^{-1} VS. For the whole experiment, the methane content of the biogas was around 65 %. COD elimination was slightly decreasing from 70 % at an OLR of 17 kg COD $\cdot$ m^{-3} $\cdot$ d^{-1} to 60 % at an OLR of more than 25 kg COD $\cdot$ m^{-3} $\cdot$ d^{-1}. Assuming that a VS elimination of 50 % to 60 % is considered close to the optimum for anaerobic degradation of solid waste and also considering the COD removal efficiency as well as the problem caused by formation of massive foam at higher loading rates and a reserve capacity for treatment of an increased amount of press water in the future, it is suggested that anaerobic digestion of press water should be operated at an OLR within the range of 13.5 to 22.5 kg COD $\cdot$ m^{-3} $\cdot$ d^{-1} (7.5 to 12.4 kg VS $\cdot$ $m^{-3} \cdot d^{-1}$).

A rough energy calculation was also performed in order to examine the energy balance in a composting plant equipped with pressing facility (energy gain from biogas and energy requirement for substrate pre-treatment and maintenance of anaerobic digestion). The result shows that the installation of an anaerobic digester to treat press water in a composting plant seems to be advantageous in terms of energy supply for a better energy balance. A net surplus energy of about 10.8 kWh may be obtained from each ton OFMSW delivered. In general, the separation of the surplus moisture from the OFMSW improves the composting process and reduces carbon dioxide emission, since a significant part of the biodegradable organic compounds is soluble and can easily be separated. The biogas from anaerobic digestion of press water can displace fossil fuel and due to greenhouse gas savings provide an environmental advantage.

Improvement of biogas production in anaerobic digestion of biowaste by co-digestion with press water and foodwaste. To optimize the existing anaerobic digesters treating OFMSW, co-digestion of other types of wastes can be considered as a strategy to maximize the renewable energy production and at the same time also optimize the municipal solid waste management. The results of the co-digestion experiment show that the addition of co-substrates (press water and foodwaste) not only increased biogas production linearly with the increment of OLRs but also improved the biogas production rates. For instance, an increase of the OLR by 10.9 % during co-digestion with press water increased the biogas production as much as 18.3% (the biogas production rate improved by 7 3 % compared to the OLR by biowaste suspension only). Similar results with slightly higher improvements were also observed during the co-digestion experiment with foodwaste.

Another interesting result was the improvement of buffer capacity of the digestate when biowaste was co-digested with press water and foodwaste. The addition of press water and foodwaste as co-substrate led to a significant increase of the digestate's buffer capacity (measured as acid capacity, $KS_{4,3}$) and enabled the operation of an anaerobic digestion without additional pH control system.

Considering the VS elimination, the improvement of biogas production as well as the potential formation of a swimming layer at the top of the reactor caused by massive foaming, the optimum addition of press water is suggested at approx. 15–20 % by volume (27-36 % in term of VS addition). The co-digestion with foodwaste gave more improvement of biogas production compared to the co-digestion with press water. However, the risk of process instabilities during co-digestion of foodwaste was also greater. At high OLRs, co-digestion with foodwaste increased the concentration of residual volatile fatty acid, which potentially disturb the process stability. Therefore, the addition of foodwaste as co-substrate is considered optimal at 10–15 % by volume (35-52 % in term of VS addition). Although the co-digestion of biowaste with presswater and foodwaste improved the yield of biogas, a special attention has to be given to the increasing soluble COD value of the wastewater resulting from the digestate dewatering process. The increase of COD value in the process water consequently increases the cost for wastewater treatment. In general, the results from this co-digestion experiment indicated that press water and foodwaste are suitable as co-substrates in anaerobic digestion of biowaste. Co-digestion with such substrates will give a higher biogas (methane) yield and improve the buffer capacity of the digestate.

Potential use of potato sludge as a co-substrate in anaerobic digestion of biowaste. Excess sludge from a wastewater treatment plant treating wastewater from the potato industry was examined in order to assess its suitability as a substrate for anaerobic digester. The concentrations of heavy metals in the potato sludge were lower than the inhibitory or toxic concentration limit. Potato sludge was also relatively easy degradable and had a maximum methane production potential of around 0.40 m^3 $CH_4 \cdot kg^{-1}$ VS_{added} achieved in approximately two weeks of incubation (more than 80% of its maximum methane production were obtained within the first 4 days of incubation). More than 70% of the volatile solid was eliminated during solid elimination tests. Judged by its relatively high methane production potential, degradability rate and solids removal potential, potato sludge is suitable for anaerobic digestion either as a sole substrate or co-substrate.

5.2   Recommendations

From the results and the experiences during this study, several recommendations can be proposed. The recommendations can be distinguished in to two parts: the practical proposal to improve the achievement from this study and also the possible application of organic solid waste in the real situation (*i.e.* a proposal for a case study) and possible future studies on anaerobic digestion of organic solid waste to enrich and to complete the information and the knowledge on anaerobic digestion of organic solid waste.

Sand sedimentation of press water. Press water had a sand content of 3.0 $mL \cdot L^{-1}$ (4.4 $g \cdot L^{-1}$). During the experiment, the sand content of press water was a problem that required a special attention. The sand content very often sedimented in the less turbulent zones of the reactor. In the laboratory-scale reactor, it "only" caused clogging of the recirculation pump and could be easily overcome. However, in full-scale digesters this problem potentially reduces the working volume and the nominal HRT of the reactor causing instabilities of the digester performance. Abrasion of pipes for recirculation with a pump was already observed in this study. In a full scale digester, the abrasion caused by sand can occur in pipe bends or moving mechanical equipment such as pump impellers and leads to failures. These problems consequently increase the maintenance costs and time loss due to reparation. Therefore, it is suggested that a sedimentation system should be applied for press water prior to its utilization as substrate or co-substrate in anaerobic digestion.

Intermittent (discontinuous) feeding. The concentration of residual VFA in the digestate can be used as a performance parameter of an anaerobic digester treating biodegradable solid waste. The accumulation of fatty acids is normally observed during start-up periods or process instabilities following increments of organic loading. As has been observed throughout this study, concentrations of VFA during semi-continuous feeding increased from almost zero on Monday to maximum values within a week on Friday. However, when the reactor was continuously fed and the concentration of VFA is neglected, the accumulation of VFA could lead to irreversible damage of the process. Therefore, although there will be a disadvantage in term of biogas production, it is recommended to feed the reactor in intermittent mode especially during start-up and adaptation period when the organic loading is increased.

Source-separation of organic solid wastes. In terms of an anaerobic digestion process, source-separation of organic solid wastes offers several advantages. Source-separated organic solid waste can be easily examined whether or not it is suitable for anaerobic digestion substrate. Another advantage of source-separated solid waste is that this kind of waste, if it is used as a co-substrate, can be adjusted to the requirement of the main substrate (*e.g.* main substrate with less nitrogen can be co-digested with nitrogen-rich source-sorted organic solid waste). Although some possible drawbacks such as its strong dependency on participation/cooperation and possible additional capital costs are obvious, the advantages are overwhelming. Therefore, source-separation of organic solid wastes should be promoted.

Anaerobic digestion with less energy input. Due to the lack of financial and technical know-how, most organic solid wastes in less developed countries are improperly treated. If this practice is continued, at a certain time, this improperly treated solid wastes will cause environmental burden. Anaerobic digestion of organic solid wastes appears to be an interesting alternative to solve the problem since its energy recovery potential offers an economic benefit. The energy and other valuable materials recovered from the process (*i.e.* compost) can be used to compensate the costs of solid waste management. However, the anaerobic digestion technology is not always applicable and beneficial due to its energy and equipment requirement. Although anaerobic digestion requires less energy input compared to an aerobic process, this technology still need energy input for pre-treatment, mixing and maintaining the digester's temperature. Therefore, it is necessary to conduct a research focusing on anaerobic digestion of organic solid wastes with less or minimum energy input (*e.g.* anaerobic digestion without temperature control, anaerobic digestion with minimal mixing, *etc.*).

Economical analysis of the processes. Biogas recovery and waste stabilization (in term of reduction of the organic content) are the main advantages of anaerobic digestion of OFMSW. Many efforts have been aimed to maximize biogas production including pre-treatment and co-digestion with other types of wastes. However, the optimum production of biogas does not reflect the optimum benefit of an anaerobic digester. Therefore, a comprehensive economical analysis has to be performed in order to define a strategy of anaerobic digestion of OFMSW. Several factors have to be taken into account in this analysis including capital and operational cost, biogas production, solids elimination, environmental costs, environmental benefits, *etc.*

Possible application of anaerobic digestion in small-scale solid waste management.
The application of anaerobic digestion of solid waste as a part of integrated solid waste management is not always centralized. In many less developed countries, where waste separation is not the custom of the community, it is quite difficult to have centralized system. In Indonesia for example, although the composition is largely organic with the portion of vegetables/putrescible materials considered to be higher than in industrialized countries (Pasang *et al.*, 2007), the application of solid waste needs an extra effort due to large amounts of impurities. Solid waste separation in Indonesia goes only well in some point sources such as agricultural industries and markets. In such a case, anaerobic digestion with some modification to improve the benefit can be applied. In Figure 4.29, a proposal for small-scale integrated solid waste management is presented to improve the benefit by installing anaerobic digester, on-site animal farm and composting plant in order to close the nutrient and energy cycle.

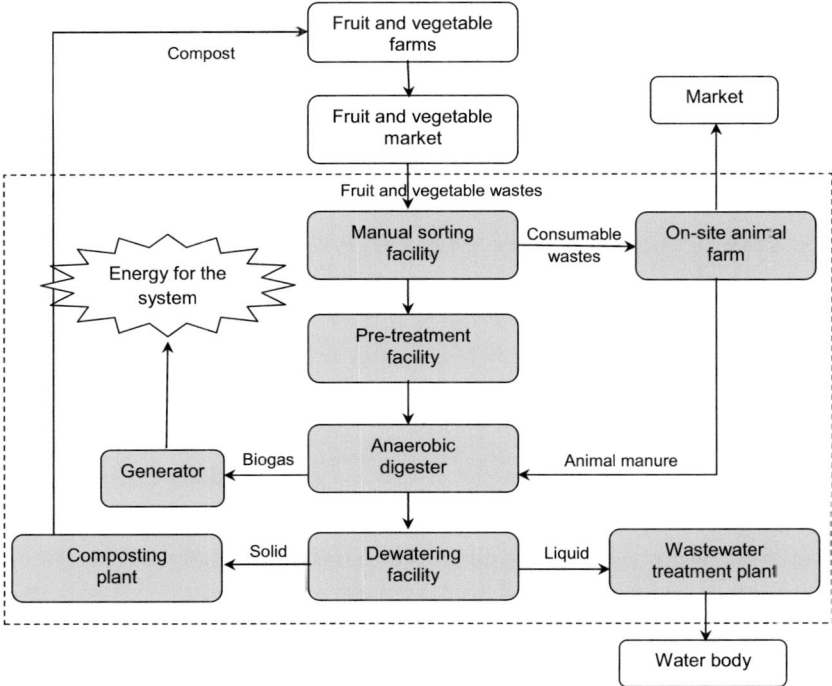

Figure 29. Small-scale plant for fruit and vegetable market solid waste.

REFERENCES

Ahring, B. K. and Westermann, P., 1983. Toxicity of heavy metals to thermophilic anaerobic digestion. *Applied microbiology and biotechnology*. Vol. 17: 365-370.

Ahring, B.K., Angelidaki, I. and Johansen, K., 1992. Anaerobic treatment of manure together with industrial waste. *Water science and technology*. Vol. 25(7): 311-318.

Alvarez, R. and Lidén, G., 2008. Semi-continuous co-digestion of solid slaughterhouse waste, manure, and fruit and vegetable waste. *Renewable energy*. Vol. 33 (4): 726-734.

Alvarez, R., and Lidén, G., 2009. Low temperature anaerobic digestion of mixtures of llama, cow and sheep manure for improved methane production. *Biomass and bioenergy*. Vol. 33: 527-533.

Angelidaki, I. and Ahring, B.K., 1993. Effect of the clay mineral bentonite on ammonia inhibition of anaerobic thermophilic reactors degrading animal waste. *Biodegradation. Vol.* 3: 409-414.

Angelidaki, I. and Ellegaard, L., 2003. Codigestion of manure and organic wastes in centralized biogas plants. *Applied biochemistry and biotechnology*. Vol. 109 (1-3): 95-105.

Angelidaki, I., Petersen, S.P., and Ahring, B. K., 1990. Effects of lipids on thermophilic anaerobic digestion and reduction of lipid inhibition upon addition of bentonite. *Applied microbiology and biotechnology*. Vol. 33 (4): 469-472.

Angelidaki, I., Ahring, B.K., 1997. Co-digestion of olive oil mill wastewaters with manure, household waste or sewage sludge. *Biodegradation*. Vol. 8: 221– 226.

Angelidaki, I., Cui, J., Chen, X. and Kaparaju, P., 2006. Operational strategies for thermophilic anaerobic digestion of organic fraction of municipal solid waste in continuously stirred tank reactors. *Environmental technology*. Vol. 27: 855-861

Appels, L., Baeyens, J., Degrève., J. and Dewil, R., 2008. Principles and potential of the anaerobic digestion of waste-activated sludge. *Progress in energy and combustion science*. Vol. 34: 755–781

Aquino, S.F., and Stuckey, D. C., 2007. Bioavailability and toxicity of metals nutrients during anaerobic digestion. Journal of *environmental engineering*. Vol. 133 (1): 28-35.

Bagchi, A., 2004. *Design of landfills and integrated solid waste management, 3rd edition*. John Wiley and Sons.

Baldasano, J.M. and Soriano, C., 2000. Emission of greenhouse gases from anaerobic digestion processes: comparison with other municipal solid waste treatments. *Water science and technology*. Vol. 41 (3): 275-282.

Banks, C.J. and Stentiford, E. I., 2007. Biodegradable municipal solid waste: biotreatment options. *Waste and resource management*. Vol. 160 (1): 11-18.

Bashir, B.H. and Matin, A., 2004. Sodium toxicity control by the use of magnesium in an anaerobic reactor. *Journal of applied science and environmental management*. Vol. 8: 17-21.

BGK (Bundesgütegemeinschaft Kompost e.V.), 2007. Gütesicherung in Deutschland: Kompostierungs- und Vergärungsanlagen. *Humuswirtschaft & Kompost* 03/2007. http://kompost.de/fileadm n/docs/Archiv/Archiv_gs/Guetesicherung_in_Deutschla ndHUKaktuell_03_2007.pdf (Retrieved: September 2008 only in German).

Bolzonella, D., Fatone, F., Pavan, P., and Cecchi, F., 2005. Anaerobic fermentation of organic municipal solid wastes for the production of soluble organic compounds. *Industrial and engineering chemistry research*. Vol. 44: 3412-3418.

Bouallagui, H., Lahdheb, H., Ben Romdan, E., Rachdi, B.and Hamdi, M., 2009. Improvement of fruit and vegetable waste anaerobic digestion performance and stability with co-substrates addition. *Journal of environmental management*. Vol. 90: 1844-1849.

Bouallagui, H., Torrijos M., Godon, J.J., Moletta, R., Ben Cheikh, R., Touhami, Y., Delgenes, J.P. and Hamdi, M., 2004. Two-phases anaerobic digestion of fruit and vegetable wastes: bioreactors performance. *Biochemical engineering*. Vol. 21: 193-197.

CADDET (Centre for analysis and dissemination of demonstrated energy technologies), 2000. *Batch anaerobic digestion of green waste in a BIOCEL converter*. Technical brochure no. 134. Available online at: http://attfle.konetic.or.kr/kinetic/xml/use/31C3A0300618.pdf

Cecchi, F., Pavan, P., Mata-Alvarez, J., Bassettit, A. and Cozzolino, C., 1991. Anaerobic digestion of municipal solid waste: thermophilic vs. mesophilic performance at high solids. *Waste management and research*. Vol. 9: 305-315.

Chavez-Vazquez, M. and Bagley, D.M., 2002. Evaluation of the performance of different anaerobic digestion technologies for solid waste treatment. *Proceedings of the 2002 joint CSCE/EWRI of ASCE International conference on environmental engineering*. Niagara Falls: Jul. 21-24, 2002. Available online at: http://gis.lrs.uoguelph.ca/AgriEnvArchives/bioenergy/download/an_dig_u_toronto _2000.pdf.

Chen, Y., Cheng; J.J. and Creamer, K.S., 2008. Inhibition of anaerobic digestion process: A review. *Bioresource technology*. Vol. 99: 4044 - 4064

Cheremisinoff, N.P., 2003. *Handbook of solid waste management and waste minimization technologies*. Burlington, MA: Elsevier Science

Cho, J.K., Park,S.C. and Chang, H.N., 1995. Biochemical methane potential and solid state anaerobic digestion of Korean food wastes. *Bioresource Technology* . Vol. 52: 245-253

Davidsson, A., Gruvberger, C., Christensen, T.H., Hansen, T.L. and Jansen, J.L.C., 2007. Methane yield in source-sorted organic fraction of municipal solid waste. *Waste management*. Vol. 27: 406-414.

de Baere, L. and Mattheeuws, B., 2008. State-of-the-art 2008 - Anaerobic digestion of solid waste. *Waste management world*. Vol. 9 (4). Available online at: www.waste-management-world.com/articles/article_display.cfm?ARTICLE_ID =339836&p=123

de Baere, L., 2000. Anaerobic digestion of solid waste: state-of-the-art. *Water science and technology*. Vol 41 (3): 283-290

de Baere, L., 2008. The DRANCO process: a dry continuous system for solid organic waste and energy crops. *Proceedings of international symposium on anaerobic dry fermentation*. Berlin: Feb. 20-22, 2008. Available online at: http://www.ows.be /pub/Dranco-Process_IBBKfeb08.pdf

Dearman, B. and Bentham, R.H., 2007. Anaerobic digestion of food waste: Comparing leachate exchange rates in sequential batch systems digesting food waste and biosolids. *Waste management*. Vol. 27: 1792-1799.

Delgenès, J.P., Penaud, V. and Moletta, R., 2003. Pretreatments for the enhancement of anaerobic digestion of solid wastes (in: *Biomethanization of the organic fraction of municipal solid wastes*. Editor: Mata-Alvarez, J.). Amsterdam: IWA publishing company.

DEV (Deutsche Einheitsverfahren), 1983. *Deutsche Einheitsverfahren zur Wasser-, Abwasser und Schlammuntersuchung.* (Standard Methods for Water, Wastewater and Sludge Analysis). Weinheim: Verlag Chemie.

Dinamarca, S., Aroca, G., Chamy, R. and Guerrero, L. 2003. The influence of pH in the hydrolytic stage of anaerobic digestion of the organic fraction of urban solid waste. *Water science and technology.* Vol. 48 (6): 249-254.

DMEE (Danish Ministry of Energy and Environment), 1996. *Energy 21: The Danish's government action plan for energy 1996.* Copenhagen. Available online at: http://193.88.185.141/Graphics/publikationer/energipolitik_uk/e21uk/contents.htm

EC (European commission), 1995. *Biogas production by treating sludge of a waste water treatment plant.* Available online at: http://ec.europa.eu/energy/renewables/bioenergy/doc/anaerobic/013bm_238_1989.pdf

EC (The Council of the European Union), 1999. *Council Directive 1999/31/EC of 26 April 1999 on the Landfill of Waste.* Official journal of the European communities L 182/1, 16/7/1999, 1999.

EC (The European Parliament and the Council of the European Union), 2009. *Directives on the promotion of the use of energy from renewable sources.* Directive 2009/28/EC: 29 April 2009.

Edelmann, W. and Engeli, H., 2005. *More than 12 years of experience with commercial anaerobic digestion of the organic fraction of municipal solid wastes in Switzerland.* Key note lecture on congress: Anaerobic digestion of solid waste (ADSW2005). Copenhagen: Aug. 31-Sept.3, 2005. Available online at: http://www.arbi.ch/ADsw.pcf

EEA (European Environment Agency), 2003. *Europe's Environment: The third assessment,* Environmental Assessment Report No 10. Kopenhagen: EEA

Eldem, N.O., Akgiray, O.M., Ozturk,I., Soyer, E. and Calli, B., 2004. Ammonia and pH inhibition in anaerobic treatment of wastewaters, part II: Model development. *Journal of environmental science and health. Part A—toxic/hazardous substances & environmental engineering.* Vol. 39 (9): 2421–2435.

Eriksson, O., Carlsson_Reich, M., Frostell, B., Björklund, A., Assefa, G., Sundqvist, J. -O., Granath, J., Baky, A. and Thyseliuz, L., 2005. Municipal solid waste management from a systems perspective. *Journal of cleaner production.* Vol. 13, Issue 3: 241-252.

Fernandes, T.V., Klaasse-Bos, G.J., Zeeman, G., Sanders, J.P.M. and van Lier, J.B., 2009. Effects of thermo-chemical pre-treatment on anaerobic biodegradability and hydrolysis of lignocellulosic biomass. *Bioresource technology*. Vol. 100: 2575-2579.

Fernández, A., Sánchez , A. and Font, X., 2005. Anaerobic co-digestion of a simulated organic fraction of municipal solid wastes and fats of animal and vegetable origin. *Biochemical engineering*. Vol. 26: 22-28.

Fountoulakis, M.S. and Manios, T., 2009. Enhanced methane and hydrogen production from municipal solid waste and agro-industrial by-products co-digested with crude glycerol. *Bioresource technology*. Vol. 100: 3043–3047

Fountoulakis, M.S., Drakopoulou, S., Terzakis, S., Georgaki, E., Manios, T., 2008. Potential for methane production from typical mediterranean agro-industrial by-products. *Biomass and bioenergy*. Vol. 32: 155–161.

Fricke, K., Santen, H. and Wallmann, R., 2005. Comparison of selected aerobic and anaerobic procedures for MSW treatment. *Waste management*. Vol. 25: 799-810.

Fruteau de Laclos, H., Desbois, S. and Saint-Joly, C., 1997. Anaerobic digestion of municipal solid organic waste: Valorga full-scale plant in Tilburg, the Netherlands. *Water science and technology*. Vol. 36 (6–7): 457–462.

Gallert, C. and Winter, J., 1997. Mesophilic and thermophilic anaerobic digestion of source-sorted organic wastes: Effect of ammonia on glucose degradation and methane production. *Applied microbiology biotechnology*. Vol.48: 405-410.

Gallert, C. and Winter, J., 1999. Bacterial metabolism in wastewater treatment systems. (In: *Biotechnology*, Vol. 11a. Series editors: Rehm, H.J., Reed, G., Pühler, A. and Stadler, P. Volume editor: Winter, J.). Weinheim: Wiley-VCH.

Gallert, C. and Winter, J., 1999. Bacterial metabolism in wastewater treatment systems. In: *Biotechnology: Environmental Processes I* . Editors.: Rehm, H.-J., Reed, G., Pühler, A.and Stadler, P. Volume editor: Winter, J. New York: Wiley, VCH.

Gallert, C. and Winter, J., 2002. Solid and liquid residues as raw materials for biotechnology. *Naturwissenschaften*. Vol. 89: 483-496.

Gallert, C. and Winter, J., 2005. *Bacterial metabolism in wastewater treatment systems* (in: Environmental biotechnology: concepts and applications. Editors: Jördening, H-J. and Winter, J.). Weinheim: Wiley-VCH.

Gallert, C. and Winter, J., 2008. Propionic acid accumulation and degradation during restart of a full-scale anaerobic biowaste digester. *Bioresource technology*. Vol. 99: 170-178.

Gallert, C., Henning, A. and Winter, J., 2003. Scale-up of anaerobic digestion of the biowaste fraction from domestic wastes. *Water research*. Vol. 37: 1433-1441.

Gallert, C., Bauer, S. and Winter, J.. 1998. Effect of ammonia on the anaerobic degradation of protein by a mesophilic and thermophilic biowaste population. Vol. 50: 495 – 501.

Gallert, C., Henning, A. and Winter, J., 2003. Scale-up anaerobic digestion of the biowaste fraction from domestic wastes. *Water research*. Vol. 37: 1433-1441

Gerardi, M.H., 2003. *The microbiology of anaerobic digesters*. Hoboken, NJ: John Wiley & sons, Inc.

Gijzen, H.J., 2002. Anaerobic digestion for sustainable development: a natural approach. *Water research and technology*. Vol. 45 (10): 321-328.

Graja, S. and Wilderer, P.A., 2001. Characterization and treatment of the liquid effluents from the anaerobic digestion of organic solid waste. *Water science and technology*. Vol .43(3): 265-274.

Haines, R., 2008. *The BTA® process*. Workshop presentation: Implementing anaerobic digestion in Wales. Nov. ' 1, 2008. Available online at: http://www.swea.co.uk/downloads/Biogas_ROBYN.pdf

Hanaki, K., Matsuo, T. and Nagase, M., 1981. Mechanism of inhibition caused by long-chain fatty acids in anaerobic digestion process. *Biotechnology and bioengineering*. Vol. 23: 1591-1610.

Hansen, T.L., Svärd, Å., Angelidaki, I., Schmidt, J.E., Jansen, J., and Christensen, T.H., 2003. Chemical characteristics and methane potentials of source-sorted and pre-treated organic municipal solid waste. *Water science and technology*. Vol. 48(4): 205-208.

Hartmann, H. and Ahring , B. K., 2006. Strategies for the anaerobic digestion of the organic fraction of municipal solid waste: an overview. *Water science and technology*. Vol. 53 (8): 7-22.

Hartmann, H. and Ahring, B. K. , 2005. A novel process configuration for anaerobic digestion of source-sorted household waste using hyper-thermophilic post-treatment. *Biotechnology and Bioengineering. Vol.* 90 (7): 830-837.

Hartmann, H. and Ahring, B. K., 2005. Anaerobic digestion of the organic fraction of municipal solid waste: influence of co-digestion with manure. *Water research.* Vol. 39: 1543-1552.

Hartmann, H. and B. K. Ahring, 2006. Strategis for the anaerobic digestion of the organic fraction of municipal solid waste: an overview. *Water science and technology.* Vol. 53 (8): 7-22.

Hartmann, H., Angelidaki, I. and Ahring, B.K., 2003. Co-digestion of the organic fraction of municipal solid waste with other waste types (in: *Biomethanization of the organic fraction of municipal solid wastes.* Editor: Mata-Alvarez, J.). Amsterdam: IWA publishing company.

Hilton, B.L. and Oleszkiewicz, J.A., 1988. Sulfide-induced inhibition of anaerobic digestion. *Journal of environmental engineering.* Vol. 114: 1377 – 1391.

Hogg, D., Barth, J., Schleiss, K. and Favoino, E., 2007. *Dealing with foodwaste in the UK.* Bristol: Eunomia Research and Consulting. Available online at: http://www.wrap.org.uk/downloads/Dealing_with_Food_Waste_-_Final_-_2_March_07.7d92e2a0.3603.pdf

Inanc, B., Matsui, S. and Ide, S., 1999. Propionic acid accumulation in anaerobic digestion of carbohydrates: an investigation on the role of hydrogen gas. *Water science and technology.* Vol. 40 (1): 93 -100.

Kaltschmitt, M. and Weber, M., 2006. Markets for solid biofuels within the EU-15. *Biomass and bioenergy.* Vol. 30: 897–907.

Kandler, O., Temper, U., Steiner, A. and Winter, J., 1983. Efficiency and stability of methane fermentation of wastes at mesophilic and thermophilic temperatures. Proceedings of the symposium on recent advances in biotechnology. New Delhi: Nov. 1, 1983.

Kaparaju, P., Buendia, I., Ellegaard, L., and Angelidaki, I., 2007. Effects of mixing on methane production during thermophilic anaerobic digestion of manure: Lab-scale and pilot-scale studies. *Bioresource technology.* Vol. 99: 4919–4928

Karagiannidis, A. and Perkoulidis, G., 2009. A multi-criteria ranking of different technologies for the anaerobic digestion for energy recovery of the organic fraction of municipal solid wastes. *Bioresource technology*. Vol. 100: 2355–2360.

Karim, K., Klasson, T., Hoffmann, R., Drescher, S. R., DePaoli, D. W., and Al-Dahhan, M.H., 2005. Anaerobic cigestion of animal waste: Effect of mixing. *Bioresource technology*. Vol. 96: 1607–1612

Kayhanian, M. and Hardy, S., 1994. The impact of four design parameters or the performance of a high-solids anaerobic digestion of municipal solid waste for fuel gas production. *Environmental technology*. Vol. 15: 557-567.

Kayhanian, M., 1999. Ammonia inhibition in high-solids biogasification: An overview and practical solutions. *Environmental technology*. Vol. 20: 355–365.

Kelleher, B.P., Leahy, J.J., Menihan, A.M., O'Dwyer, T.F., Sutton, D. and Leahy, M.J., Advances in poultry litter disposal technology – a review. *Bioresource technology*. Vol. 83 (1): 27 - 36.

Kim, H.W., Han, S.K. and Shin, H.S., 2003. The optimisation of food waste addition as a co-substrate in anaerobic digestion of sewage sludge. *Waste management and research*. Vol. 21: 515-526.

Kim, J.K., Han, G.H., Oh, B.R., Chun, Y.N., Eom, C.Y. and Kim, S.W., 2008. Volumetric scale-up of a three stage fermentation system for food waste treatment . *Bioresource technology*. Vol. 99:4394–4399

Kim, J.K., Oh, B.R., Chun, Y.R. and Kim, S.W., 2006. Effects of temperature ard hydraulic retention time on anaerobic digestion of food waste. *Journal of bioscience and bioengineering*. Vol. 102 (4): 328-332.

Knezevic, Z., 1995. Pilot-scale evaluation of anaerobic co-digestion of primary and pretreated waste activated sludge. *Water and environmental research*. Vol.67:835–41.

Kobya, M., Hiz, H., Senturk, E., Aydiner, C. And Demirbas, E., 2006. Treatment of potato chips manufacturing wastewater by electrocoagulation. *Desalination*. Vol. 190: 201-211.

KOMPOGAS AG., 2007. *Mechanical-biological waste treatment based on the KOMPOGAS process*. Available online at: http://*www.kompogas.com/uploads/media /e_mba_2007_01.pdf*

Koppar, A. and Pullammanappallil, P., 2008. Single-stage, batch, leach-bed, thermophilic anaerobic digestion of spent sugar beet pulp. *Bioresources technology*. Vol. 99 (8): 2831-2839.

Kouzeli-Katsiri, A., and Kartsonas, N., 1986. Inhibitory of anaerobic digestion by heavy metals, in: *Anaerobic digestion of sewage sludge and organic agricultural wastes* (Bruce, A.M., Konzeli-Katsiri, A., and Newman, P.J., Eds.), 104-119. Elsevier Applied Science Publisher, London, UK.

Kouzeli-Katsiri, A., Kartsonas, N. and Priftis, A., 1988. Assessment of the toxicity of heavy metals to the anaerobic digestion of sewage sludge. *Environmental technology*. Vol. 9 (4): 261-270.

Krogmann, U., 1999. Effects of season and population density on source-separated waste composts. *Waste management & research*. Vol. 17: 109-123.

Krogmann, U., and Körner, I., 2000. Technology and strategies of composting. In *Biotechnology, Vol. 11c* (Series editors: Rehm, H.J., Reed, G., Pühler, A. and Stadler, P., Volume editors: Klein, J. and Winter, J.). Weinheim, Germany: Wiley-VCH.

Krzystek, L., Ledakowicz, S., Kahle, H.J. and Kaczorek, K., 2001. Degradation of household biowaste in reactors. *Biotechnology*. Vol. 92: 103-112.

Kübler, H. ,1996. Anfall und reinigung von Abwasser bei der Vergärung von Bioabfall. *Korrespondenz Abwasser*. Vol. 5: 796–808.

Kübler, H., Hoppenheidt, K., Hirsch, P., Kottmair, A., Nimmrichter, R., Nordsieck, H., Mücke, W. and Swerev, M., 2000. Full scale co-digestion of organic waste. *Water science and technology*. Vol. 41 (3): 195-202.

Lay, J-J., Li, Y-Y., and Noike, T., 1998. The influence of pH and ammonia concentration on the methane production in high-solids digestion processes. *Water environment research*. Vol. 70 (5): 1075-1082.

Lee, G. F. and Jones-Lee, A., 1999. *Unreliability of predicting landfill gas production rates and duration for closed subtitle D MSW landfills*. Report of G. Fred Lee & Associates, El Macero, CA. Available online at: http://www.gfredlee.com/ Landfills/lf_gas_paper.pdf

Lissens, G., Vandevivere, P., De Baere, L., Biey, E.M. and Verstraete, W., 2001. Solid waste digestors: process performance and practice for municipal solid waste digestion. *Water science and technology*. Vol 44 (8): 91-102.

López-Torres, M. and Espinosa-Lloréns, M. d. C., 2008. Effect of alkaline pretreatment on anaerobic digestion of solid wastes. *Waste management*. Vol. 28 (11): 2229-2234.

Luning, L., van Zundert, E.H.M., and Brinkmann, A.J.F., 2003. Comparison of dry and wet digestion for solid waste. *Water science and technology*. Vol 48 (4): 15-20.

Macias-Corral, M., Samani, Z., Hanson, A., Smith, G., Funk, P., Yu, H. and Longworth, J., 2008. Anaerobic digestion of municipal solid waste and agricultural waste and the effect of co-digestion with dairy cow manure. *Bioresource technology*. Vo. 99 (17): 8288-8293.

Malladi, B. and Ingham, S.C., 1993. Thermophilic aerobic treatment of potato-processing wastewater. *World journal of microbiology and biotechnology*. Vol. 9: 43-49.

Maroun, R. and El Fadel, M., 2007. Start-up of anaerobic digestion of source-sorted organic municipal solid waste in the absence of classical inocula. *Environmental science and technology*. Vol. 41: 6808-6814.

Mata-Alvarez, J., 2002. Fundamentals of the anaerobic digestion process (in: *Biomethanization of the organic fraction of municipal solid wastes*. Editor: Mata-Alvarez, J.). Amsterdam: IWA publishing company.

Mata-*Alvarez*, J., Macé, S. and Llabrés, P., 2000. Anaerobic digestion of organic solid wastes: an overview of research achievements and perspectives. *Bioresource technology*. Vol. 74: 3 – 16.

Mato, S., Otero, D. and Garcia, M., 1994. Composting of < 100 mm fraction of municipal solid waste. *Waste management & research*. Vol. 12: 315-325.

McCarty, P.L. and McKinney, R.E., 1961. Salt toxicity in anaerobic digestion. *Journal of water pollution control federation*. Vol. 33 (4): 399-415.

McCarty, P.L. and Mosey, F.E., 1991. Modelling of anaerobic digestion processes. *Water science and technology*. Vol. 24 (8): 17-33.

Meroney, R.N. and Colorado, P.E., 2009. CFD simulation of mechanical draft tube mixing in anaerobic digester tanks. *Water research*. Vol. 43: 1040–1050

Metcalf & Eddy, Inc., 2003. *Wastewater engineering: Treatment and reuse*. 4th ed. New York: McGraw-Hill.

Miah, M.S., Tada, C., Yang, Y. and Sawayama, S., 2005. Aerobic thermophilic bacteria enhance biogas production. *Journal of material cycles and waste management.* Vol. 7: 48-54.

Mishra, B.K., Arora, A. and Lata, 2004. Optimization of a biological process for treating potato chips industry wastewater using a mixed culture of *Aspergillus foetidus* and *Aspergillus niger. Bioresource technology.* Vol. 94 (1): 9-12.

Mosier, N., Wyman, C., Dale, B., Elander, R., Lee, Y.Y, Holtzapple, M. and Ladisch, M., 2005. Features of promising technologies for pretreatment of lignocellulosic biomass. *Bioresource technology.* Vol. 96 (6): 673-686.

Mshandete, A., Björnsson, L., Kivaisi, A.K., Rubindamayugi, M.S.T., and Mattiasson, B., 2006. Effect of particle size on biogas yield from sisal fibre waste. *Renewable energy.* Vol. 31: 2385 – 2392.

Mshandete, A., Kivaisi, A., Rubindamayugi, M. and Mattiasson, B., 2004. Anaerobic batch co-digestion of sisal pulp and fish wastes. *Bioresource technology.* Vol. 95: 19–24.

Mtz.-Viturtia, A., Mata-Alvarez, J. and Cecchi, F., 1995. Two-phase continuous anaerobic digestion of fruit and vegetable wastes. *Resources, conservation and recycling.* Vol. 13: 257-267.

Murphy, J.D. and McKeogh, E., 2004. Technical, economic and environmental analysis of energy production from municipal solid waste. *Renewable energy.* Vol. 29: 1043-1057.

Murto, M., Björnsson, L. and Mattiasson B., 2004. Impact of food industrial waste on anaerobic co-digestion of sewage sludge and pig manure. *Journal of environmen management.* Vol. 70: 101–107.

Neves, L., Gonçalo, E., Oliveira, R. and Alves, M.M., 2008. Influence of composition on the biomethanation potential of restaurant waste at mesophilic temperatures. *Waste management.* Vol. 28: 965-972.

Nichols, C.E., 2004. Overview of anaerobic digestion technologies in Europe. *BioCycle.* Vol. 45 (1): 47.

Nishio, N and Nakashimada, Y., 2007. Recent development of anaerobic digestion processes for energy recovery from wastes. *Journal of bioscience and bioengineering.* Vol. 103 (29): 105–112.

Nordberg, A. and M. Edström, 2005. Co-digestion of energy crops and the source-sorted organic fraction of municipal solid waste. *Water science and technology*. Vol. 52 (1-2): 217-222.

Nordberg, Å., and Edström, M., 2005. Co-digestion of energy crops and the source-sorted organic fraction of municipal solid waste. *Water science and technology*. Vol. 52 (1-2): 217-222.

OECD (Organisation for economic co-operation and development), 2004. Towards waste prevention performance indicators. Available online at: http://www.olis.oecd.org/olis/2004doc.nsf/LinkTo/NT00007B3E/$FILE/JT0017044 2.PDF

Oleszkiewicz, J.A. and Sharma, V.K., 1990. Stimulation and inhibition of anaerobic processes by heavy metals - A review. *Biological wastes*. Vol. 3: 45-67.

Palmisano, A.C. and Barlaz, M.A., 1996. *Microbiology of solid waste*. Boca Raton, Florida: CRC Press Inc.

Palmowski, L.M. and Müller, J.A., 2000. Influence of the size reduction of organic waste on their anaerobic digestion. *Water science and technology*. Vol. 41 (3): 155–162.

Palmowski, L.M. and Müller, J.A., 2000. Influence of the size reduction of organic waste on their anaerobic digestion. *Water science and technology*. Vol. 41 (3): 155–162.

Palmowski, L.M. and Müller, J.A., 2003. Anaerobic degradation of organic materials - significance of the substrate surface area. *Water science and technology*. Vol. 47 (12): 231-238.

Pasang, H., Moore, G.A. and Sitorus, G., 2007. Neighbourhood-based waste management: A solution for solid waste problems in Jakarta, Indonesia. Waste management. Vol. 27: 1924-1938.

Pavlosthatis, S.G. and Giraldo-Gomez, E., 1991. Kinetics of anaerobic treatment. *Water science and technology*. Vol. 24 (8): 35-59.

Renkow, M. and Rubin, A.R., 1998. Does municipal solid waste composting make economic sense? *Environmental management*. Vol. 53 (4): 339-357.

Residua, 2009, *Information sheet on anaerobic digestion of solid waste*. Available online at (last access June 2009): http://www.waste.nl/content/download/472/ 3779/file/WB89-InfoSheet(Anaerobic% 20 Digestion).pdf

Rincón, B., Borja, R., González, J.M., Portillo, M.C. and Sáiz-Jiménez, C., 2008. Influence of organic loading rate and hydraulic retention time on the performance, stability and microbial communities of one-stage anaerobic digestion of two-phase olive mill solid residue. *Biochemical engineering*. Vol. 40: 253-261.

Rodriguez-Iglesias, J., Castrillón Pelaez, L., Marañon Maison, E., and Sastre Andres H., 2000. Biomethanization of municipal solid waste in a pilot plant. *Water research*. Vol. 34(2): 447-454.

Salhofer, S., Obersteiner, G., Schneider, F., and Lebersorger, S., 2007. Potentials for the prevention of municipal solid waste. *Waste management*. Vol. 28: 245-259.

Salminen, E.A. and Rintala, J.A., 2002. Semi-continuous anaerobic digestion of solid poultry slaughterhouse waste: effect of hydraulic retention time and loading. *Water research*. Vol. 36: 3175-3182.

Sanchez, J.M., Valle, L., Rodriguez, F., Moriñigo, M.A. and Borrego, J.J., 1996. Inhibition of methanogenesis by several heavy metals using pure cultures. *Letters in applied microbiology*. Vol. 23: 439 – 444.

Schober, G. Schäfer, J., Schmid-Staiger, U. and Trösch, W., 1999. One and two-stage digestion of solid organic waste. *Water research*. Vol. 33 (3): 854 – 860.

Schu, K. and Schu, R., 2007. *Waste fermentation and sand – no problem?*. 2. Internationale Tagung MBA. Hannover: May 22 – 24, 2007.

Slater, R.A. and Frederickson, J., 2001. Composting municipal waste in the UK: some lessons from Europe. *Resources, conservation & recycling*. Vol. 32: 359–374.

Sosnowski, P., Wieczorek, A. and Ledakowicz, S., 2003. Anaerobic co-digestion of sewage sludge and organic fraction of municipal solid wastes. *Advance environmental research*. Vol. 7: 609–616.

Stabnikova, O., Liu, X.Y. and Wang, J.Y., 2008. Digestion of frozen/thawed food waste in the hybrid anaerobic solid–liquid system. *Waste management*. Vol. 28: 1654-1659.

Statistisches Bundesamt, 2008a. *Erhebung über Haushaltsabfälle: Ergebnisbericht 2006*. Wiesbaden, Germany: Statistisches Bundesamt.

Statistisches Bundesamt, 2008b. *Abfallentsorgung 2006, Fachserie 19 Reihe 1*. Wiesbaden, Germany: Statistisches Bundesamt.

Stronach, S. M., Rudd, T., and Lester, J. N., 1986. *Anaerobic digestion processes in wastewater treatment*. Berlin: Springer.

Stroot, P.G., McMahon, K.D., Mackie, R.I.,and Raskin, L., 2001. Anaerobic codigestion of municipal solid waste and biosolids under various mixing condition: I. Digester performance. *Water research*. Vol. 24 (7): 1804-1816.

Sung, S. and Liu, T., 2003. Ammonia inhibition on thermophilic anaerobic digestion. *Chemosphere*. Vol. 53: 43-52.

Takashima, M. and Speece, R.E., 1989. Mineral nutrient requirements for high rate methane fermentation of acetate at low SRT. *Research journal of the water pollution control federation*. Vol. **61** (11–12): 1645–1650.

Temper, U., Winter, J., and Kandler, O., 1983. Methane fermentation of wastes at mesophilic and thermophilic temperatures (In: *Energy from biomass-2nd E.C. Conference*. Editors: Strub, A., Chartier, P. and Schleser, G.). London and New York: Appl. Sci. Publ. Page: 521-525.

ten Brummeler, E., 2000. Full scale experience with the BIOCEL process. *Water science and technology*. Vol. 41 (3): 299-304.

Trzcinski, A.P. and Stuckey, D.C., 2009. Continuous treatment of the organic fraction of municipal solid waste in an anaerobic two-stage membrane process with liquid recycle. *Water research*. Vol. 43: 2449-2462.

UNFPA (United Nations Fund for Population Activities), 2007. State of world population 2007: Unleashing the potential of urban growth. Available online at: http://www.unfpa.org/swp/2007/english/introduction.html.

United Nations, 2007. *World Population Prospects - The 2006 Revision* , New York: Population Division, Department of Economic and Social Affairs, United Nations Available online at: http://www.un.org/esa/population/publications/ wpp2006/WPP2006_Highlights_rev.pdf.

US-EPA (Environmental Protection Agency), 2002. *Waste not, want not: feeding the hungry and reducing solid waste through food recovery, EPA 530-R-99-040*. National Service Center for Environmental Publications. Available online at: http://www.epa.gov/waste/conserve/materials/organics/pubs/wast_not.pdf

van Haandel, A.C., Monroy, O., Celis, B., Rustrian, E. and Cervantes, F.J., 2005. Principles of process design in industrial wastewater treatment system. In: *Advanced biological treatment processes for industrial wastewaters (Eds.: Cervantes, F.J., Pavlostathis, S.G. and van Haandel, A.C.).* London: IWA Publishing.

Vandevivere, P., De Baere, L. and Verstraete, W., 2003. Types of anaerobic digesters for solid wastes (in: *Biomethanization of the organic fraction of municipal solid wastes.* Editor: Mata-Alvarez, J.). Amsterdam: IWA publishing company.

Vandevivere, P., L. De Baere and W. Verstraete, 2002. Types of anaerobic digesters for solid wastes (in: *Biomethanization of the organic fraction of municipal solid wastes,* J. Mata-Alvarez-ed.), Amsterdam: IWA

Vavilin, V.A, Rytov, S.V., Pavlostathis, S.G., Jokela J. and J. Rintala, 2003. A distributed model of solid waste anaerobic digestion: sensitivity analysis. *Water science and technology.* Vol .48(4): 147-154.

Veeken, A., Kalyuzhnyi, S., Scharff,H., and Hamelers, B., 2000. Effect of pH and VFA on hydrolysis of organic solid waste. *Journal of environmental engineering.* Vol. 126 (12): 1076 – 1081.

Veenstra, S., 2000. *Wastewater treatment I.* Delft: International Institute for Infrastructure, Hydraulics and Environmental Engineering (IHE Delft).

Wang, J.Y., Xu H.L. and Tay J. H., 2002. A hybrid two-phase system for anaerobic digestion of food waste. *Water science and technology.* Vol. 45 (12): 159 -165.

Wang, Y.S., Odle III, W.S., Eleazer, W.E. and Bariaz, M.A., 1997. Methane potential of food waste and anaerobic toxicity of leachate produced during food waste decomposition. *Waste management & research.* Vol. 15: 149- 167.

Williams, R. B., Jenkins, B. M., and Nguyen, D., 2003. *Solid waste conversion: a review and database of current and emerging technologies.* Department of Biological and Agricultural Engineering, University of California at Davis: Final report for California integrated waste management board.

Winter J., Temper, U., Steiner, A. and Kandler, O., 1982. Biogaspotential, Prozeßstabilität und Hygienisierung bei der mesophilen und thermophilen Vergärung von Schlämmen (In: *2. Biogasfachgespräch.* Editor: Baader, W.). Braunschweig: Institut für Technologie der FAL.

Wittmann, C. , Zeng, A.P., Deckwer, W.D., 1995. Growth inhibition by ammonia and use of pH-controlled feeding strategy for the effective cultivation of *Mycobacterium chlorophenolicum*. *Applied microbiology and biotechnology.* Vol. 44: 519-525.

Wolf, P. and Nordmann, W. 1977. *Eine Feldmethode für die Messung des CSB von Abwasser.* (A field method for COD analysis in wastewater). *Korespondenz Abwasser.* Vol. 24: 277-279.

Wu, G., Healy, M.G. and Zhan, X., 2009. Effect of the solid content on anaerobic digestion of meat and bone meal. *Bioresource Technology* . Vol. 100: 4326-4331.

Zaher, U., Cheong, D-Y., Wu,B., and Chen, S., *Producing energy and fertilizer from organic municipal solid waste.* Olympia, WA: Department of Biological Systems Engineering, WSU. Also available online at: http://www.ecy.wa.gov/programs/ swfa/solidwastedata/

Zaher, U., Li, R., Jeppsson, U., Steyer, J.P. and Chen, S., 2009. GISCOD: General integrated solid waste co-digestion model. *Water research.* Vol. 43: 2717-2727

Zhang, B., Zhang, L.L., Zhang, S.C., Shi, H.Z. and Cai, W.M., 2005. The influence of pH on hydrolysis and acicogenesis of kitchen wastes in two-phase anaerobic digestion. *Environmental technology.* Vol. 26: 329-339.

Zhang, R., El-Mashad, H.M., Hartman, K., Wang, F., Liu, G., Choate, C. and Gamble, P., 2007. Characterization of food waste as feedstock for anaerobic digestion. *Bioresources technology.* Vol. 98: 929-935.

Zupančič, G.D., Uranjek-Ževart, N. and Roš, M., 2008. Full-scale anaerobic co-digestion of organic waste and municipal sludge. *Biomass and bioenergy.* Vol. 32: 163-167.